THE MARKET

THE MARKET

MATTHEW WATSON

To the wonderful NHS staff at the Queen Elizabeth Hospital Birmingham, for putting Katie back together again. If ever there was a place where the political discourse of "the market" really should not be allowed …

First published in 2018 by Agenda Publishing

Agenda Publishing Limited
The Core
Science Central
Bath Lane
Newcastle upon Tyne
NE4 5TF
www.agendapub.com

ISBN 978-1-911116-60-8 (hardcover)
ISBN 978-1-911116-61-5 (paperback)

British Library Cataloguing-in-Publication Data
A catalogue record for this book is available from the British Library

Typeset by JS Typesetting Ltd, Porthcawl, Mid Glamorgan
Printed and bound in the UK by TJ International

CONTENTS

ACKNOWLEDGEMENTS

This book has been written relatively quickly, but the ideas on which it is based have had a much longer gestation period.

I first became politically aware in my early teenage years, in the midst of the long UK recession of the early 1980s. During that time, we had careers classes at school on how to deal with unemployment, so assured did it seem that "the market" had taken away the types of job that my class and I would be most likely to do. The later teenage me watched as the Berlin Wall came down at the end of the 1980s, and I listened to commentators say that "the market" had helped western capitalism to win the Cold War. Whilst I was writing my PhD in the mid-to-late 1990s, the world was abuzz with talk of globalization. We were told that "the market", now suitably expanded spatially to become a truly global phenomenon, would bring us riches that we could never previously even have dreamt of. But the cost was that we must accept that it would no longer permit us to think politically about modes of social organization that differed markedly from the status quo. Latterly, we have had the global financial crisis, which started at roughly the time that I was awarded my first professorial position. I watched in horror as one market after another imploded, and I watched in horror again as the poorest members of society were made to fund the clean-up operation, because austerity – apparently – was the only policy response that "the market" would allow.

The me today is no less puzzled than was the teenage me by the political work that can be done when deference to "the market" construct is secured. I am perhaps capable of exhibiting a higher-functioning level of bewilderment now than I was back in the early 1980s, but the temptation to knot my brow and let out an exasperated sigh is just the same. Every time I hear a politician declare confidently that there are only so many things that "the market" will bear, I offer an identical response. "What is this thing called 'the market' to which you refer?" I ask myself. Often I hear the opinion of an economist being cited in support of the argument that, like it or not, we must all bow to the will of "the market". But I have learnt enough about economic theory during my life to know that, on its own, it can never be the source of the political discourse of "the market". The two exist on their own planes of thought. They make claims about the world that are simply too different for economists' market concept to ever act unproblematically as support for politicians who use their discourse of "the market" as a smokescreen for creating an ever more inegalitarian society.

The chapters that now lie in front of you have been written to explore this essential difference, something that has been bubbling around in my mind for so long. It is all-too-easy to think that you are hearing the same thing when economists explain their market concept as when politicians appeal to their discourse of "the market". After all, the single word "market" is necessarily going to be the mainstay of both. However, much can be gained from resisting the temptation to conflate the two. Economists' market concept should be judged on its own terms, the political discourse of "the market" likewise. Still, though, the conflation of the two is an important element of the contemporary political environment. I have therefore reserved a good proportion of my commentary for exploring the points at which the leap seems to have been made from the market concept to market ideology.

This book has been written with financial assistance from the UK's Economic and Social Research Council. Between 2013 and 2018 I held one of its Professorial Fellowships to support my "Rethinking the Market" project (www.warwick.ac.uk/rethinkingthemarket). I have been sufficiently lucky to have been in receipt of ESRC funding at various points in my career, and the most recent period of funding – Grant Award Number ES/K010697/1 – has helped me enormously to clarify lots of important conceptual issues that have been in the background of my work for a long time now. This book represents some of that effort falling into place, allowing me to make more systematic sense of innumerable conversations I have had with students and colleagues over the years. I am very grateful to all these people, for they have helped to shape my thinking in ways that they will never know. I am also very grateful to the ESRC for the continuing faith that it has shown in my research, and for its willingness to back that faith with public money.

I also owe a very large debt of gratitude to my publishers at Agenda, Alison Howson and Steven Gerrard. They have been wonderful to work with: always encouraging, always willing to give me my head provided I could explain what it was that I was trying to do, always trusting that I would come good on my promises, and always with a sharp eye for new features that might improve the text. They have been exemplary in the support that they have offered to me, and the book would be noticeably the worse without it.

As always, my biggest thanks come last and they go to Katie.

Matthew Watson

CHAPTER 1

INTRODUCTION

THE POWER OF "THE MARKET"

"The historical debate is over. The answer is free-market capitalism."

Thomas Friedman, *New York Times* columnist and
three-time Pullitzer Prize winner

"You can't buck the market."

Margaret Thatcher, UK Prime Minister, 1979–90

In May 1981 François Mitterrand was elected President of France, the first Socialist Party President of the Fifth Republic. The Socialists then gained a handsome parliamentary majority in a legislative election held just six weeks later, enabling Mitterrand to enact the radical programme for government on which he was elected. This was the so-called "Cent Dix Propositions pour la France" (Cole 1994: 35). The sixteenth to thirty-fifth propositions largely covered economic policy, attempting to create new sources of domestic demand that would lead to high levels of job creation. Mitterrand's egalitarian instincts saw him use the tax system to redistribute income from the wealthiest to the least wealthy members of society. The real value of transfer payments rose significantly, the minimum wage likewise, workers were given the right to more paid leave and the length of the standard working week was capped at a much lower level than previously (Tiersky 2003: 133). The Socialist leader's political popularity remained sufficiently strong for him to win the next presidential election in 1988 with a substantially enlarged majority, and the French electorate never voted down his reform programme. However, Mitterrand made a spectacular U-turn just two years into it, compelled to give up on his dream of a more equal society, it appeared, by pressure on the French franc making it more difficult for him to execute his European policy of ever deeper integration (Dyson & Featherstone 1998: 92; Callaghan 2000:

107; Parsons 2003: 170). So the conventional account of this episode has it, "the market" forced him into a significant change of heart.

In July 1997 the monetary authorities of Thailand decided to allow their country's currency, the baht, to find its own price level on global foreign exchange markets. Later that month the monetary authorities of the Philippines, Malaysia, Indonesia and South Korea took exactly the same decision (Griffith-Jones 1998: 4). All had been under ferocious attack from the selling strategies of speculators, who had bet enormous sums of money on being able to break East Asian currency pegs so that "the market" might instead determine the price of the national currency (Singh 1999: 23; Kim 2000: 101; Grabel 2003: 324). This was the **pegged exchange rate regime** that had served the cause of economic development so effectively throughout the prior three decades that it had the World Bank revelling in the success of what became known as the East Asian "tigers". However, the ensuing financial crisis dramatically reversed the preceding developmental profile across the region, being responsible for 80 million new cases of absolute poverty in the half-year to January 1998 (Stiglitz 2002: 92). To take the most extreme example, for every US$6 of consumption possibilities the Indonesian rupiah could facilitate at world prices immediately before the crisis, a barely believable US$5 was lost in that single six-month period. Nobody in Indonesia ever voted for the change in policy or the effects that ensued. Voters were also entirely bypassed as a new economic model more to the liking of foreign exchange market speculators was introduced in the other crisis-hit countries. Instead, the popular memory presents this as another instance in which "the market" simply got its way.

In July 2007 the US investment bank Bear Stearns reported that two of its largest hedge funds had no means of meeting their liabilities. These funds were overloaded with investments linked to the process of mortgage securitization (Bamber & Spencer 2008: 45; Greenberg 2010: 187). This is the act of bundling together large numbers of personal mortgage repayments into single securities that supposedly removed the risk to the investor of any individual instance of mortgage default. However, these new financial instruments did not take adequately into account the adverse effects of falling house prices on the ability of those who had been sold the riskiest mortgages to stay in their homes. Bear Stearns was consequently left with masses of non-performing loans on its books. By the time that US authorities engineered a largely private sector bailout of its remaining business in the spring of 2008, it was left carrying US$30 billion of complicated "level three" assets tied to mortgages that had been sold to people who had little chance of ever paying them off in full (Davidoff 2009: 138; Dowd & Hutchinson 2010: 312). These are assets that under normal accounting procedures have what is technically known as "unobservable" input values (Valentine 2010: 207). That is, nobody can say for sure why they should ever have traded at their pre-crisis price other than for the fact that somebody had been willing to pay it. "The market" had tolerated those asset prices for as long as the accompanying bubble in house prices remained inflated, but as soon as the bubble burst it moved to reveal the lack of judgement in the initial investments made by the Bear Stearns hedge funds.

All three of these events have entered the political consciousness as evidence of the power of "the market". In particular, this is the power to punish ostensibly errant actors. The question that immediately comes to mind is how arbitrary the retribution of "the market" seems to be, whether or not it is possible to identify clear patterns in the correctives that it imposes. (1) Mitterrand's U-turn occurred in the context of market-based suspicions of policies that were deemed to be too pro-worker, too pro-poor or, in short, too left-wing. Studies of the narrowing of party political choice under conditions of economic globalization in the 1990s and 2000s appear to confirm that Mitterrand's experience was merely a portent of things to come for the parliamentary left (Hay & Wincott 2012). (2) The Asian financial crisis has also been presented in the academic literature as a punishment for trying to follow the "wrong" type of policies. On this occasion, it was less about the position that a democratically-elected government had chosen to take on the traditional left–right party political spectrum, so much as the broad model of economic development that the country as a whole had followed in preceding decades (Sharma 2003). The interests embedded in that development model departed from those that were embedded both in western capitalism and in western economic opinion as advocated at that time by the institutions of global governance. (3) It is only really the third of the examples where we see something different. Bear Stearns was definitely not punished for the political stance it had taken, having been a poster child over many years for the new turbo version of free market capitalism (Cohan 2009). It had erred instead in misreading market signals, ploughing money that it held only on credit into investments that ultimately proved to be worthless, and finding itself on the wrong side of subsequent price movements (Kelly 2009). "The market", it seems, also exacts retribution on its own. This might not be as well developed a habit as punishing those who seek a political space beyond market logic, but it is worth remembering that those who live by "the market" can also sometimes die by it.

However, what does it mean to talk about market institutions in this way? What images of those institutions must we be appealing to – whether consciously or, more likely, not – before it makes sense to think that "the market" is something that we should avoid antagonizing for fear that it will bite us if we do? Moreover, what relationship does this image have to the market concept that is such an important part of academic economics? There were certainly lots of academic economists who were more than happy to venture the opinion that Mitterrand's Socialist Government, the crisis-hit countries of East Asia and Bear Stearns all only had themselves to blame for wilfully transgressing obvious realities of operating within the market environment. They also had their academic models to show that this was so. Does this mean, then, that the political discourse of "the market" and academic economists' market concept are merely two sides of the same coin? These are the issues that I set out to tackle in this book.

THE PROBLEM

"The only place you see a free market is in the speeches of politicians."

Dwayne Andreas, prominent US political donor

"The crisis of modern democracy is a profound one. Free elections, a free press and an independent judiciary mean little when the free market has reduced them to commodities available on sale to the highest bidder ... Democracy no longer means what it was meant to. It has been taken back into the workshop. Each of its institutions has been hollowed out, and it has been returned to us as a vehicle for the free market, of the corporations. For the corporations, by the corporations."

Arundhati Roy, Booker Prize winning author

Let me begin with the political language of "the market". It is a language that so many of us use so often in everyday speech that it is very easy to forget exactly what sort of image we are appealing to when making that language do political work for us. This is as true for critics of pro-market policies as it is of supporters. Each in their own way is likely to reinforce the same underlying image but without necessarily being conscious that this is what they are doing. What we encounter today as the political language of "the market" is typically based upon a cleverly disguised misinvocation of cause and effect. Market institutions are almost always described in terms of a bodily presence, as if market institutions themselves have free will to act upon the broader economic environment and, in turn, to shape everyday experiences of the economy in decisive ways. Whether jobs are outsourced from the national economy (A. Ross 2007), workers are forced to reduce their wage demands in an attempt to price themselves back into their jobs (Ryner 2002) or firms enrich their shareholders by reducing their labour costs in either of these ways (Stout 2012), the same causal mechanism tends to be summoned. In each of these instances, as well as in countless others besides, we are likely to be told that the observed outcome is the one that "the market" decreed. In this account of economic reality, "the market" acts and the rest of us are required to accommodate ourselves passively to the consequences of these actions. It is market institutions themselves rather than the people who operate within them that select winners and losers, rewarding the fortunate few but punishing the remainder. "Ours is not to reason why" might very well be the mantra of this political rhetoric of "the market".

Think back to your instinctive response when you were taken through the three examples with which the discussion began. If you were nodding along in silent recognition then even if entirely unknowingly you were also reproducing that mantra. The misinvocation of cause and effect in the political language of "the market" spreads far and wide. It is now assumed by ever more people in an increasingly matter-of-fact manner that "the market" has an essence as a thing that makes it capable of laying down its own rules of engagement. It is as if "the market" stalks every decision that is made about how to govern the economy, preying upon decision-makers who do not instinctively share its vision of the world, and standing by to impose corrective action on those who are deemed to have transgressed the future it is attempting to will into being. "**Thingification**" is not a word that is in common use except within some of the lesser-explored niches of the academic literature. However, it captures neatly one of the core characteristics of the political language games through which the economic world is today rendered comprehensible in everyday terms. "The market" has been turned in political speech into a thing that thinks and acts for itself (Watson 2005a: 163–8).

There is a problem to try to unravel here, because the market (this time without the inverted commas) also exists as a concept. Indeed, it could well be said that it exists in the first instance solely as a concept (Slater & Tonkiss 2001). In this guise it is an abstraction that has to be lifted out of the pages of economic theory if it is to enter political debates. Therein it connotes in its modern-day form a purely hypothetical realm that would arise in a situation in which every economic interaction is produced on the basis of voluntarily contracted exchange alone (Beckstein 2016). In other words, it is a world in which politics can safely be assumed away because there is no need for it to be there. In the hypothetical realm in which the market concept is active, everybody instinctively recognizes everybody else's right to equal treatment, and therefore there are no power asymmetries on which adjudications have to be made on behalf of society as a whole. The market concept thus refers to a utopia, a wouldn't-it-be-lovely-if-life-was-really-like-that state of affairs in which we were free to concentrate on matters of pure economic efficiency because we can rule out by definition the possibility of one person's actions causing harm to someone else (Schönpflug 2008).

Nobody, though, who has seen their job move overseas, who has been forced to try to price themselves back into work, or who has paused for a moment's reflection on the nature of global inequality, will ever delude themselves that the world is actually like this. They will be only too well aware of all of these economic harms, as well as the fact that such adverse consequences represent just the tip of the iceberg. Moreover, they are likely to have spent their lives listening to politicians say that, regrettable though some of these effects may be, they result merely from the playing out of the logic of "the market" (this time with the inverted commas again restored). Whereas the market concept implies a pristine state of social affairs in which no political entity is needed to adjudicate on who gets what because everyone gets their fair share, it is increasingly common these days to hear that "the market" has replaced the state as the adjudicator-of-last-resort of who can lay claim to the life that they most want to lead (Tanzi 2011). That is, it is "the market" that gets to express its opinion on how much inequality will be allowed to enter into the exchange relation and how much exploitation is permissible in society more generally. Indeed, considerable political effort has been expended by governments in recent decades to enforce the view that their opinion now ranks second on these issues to that of "the market" (Hudson 2012). This is all about the spreading of harms that the thought experiments enabled by the market concept simply preclude as a possibility, but that the political rhetoric of "the market" treats as a necessary aspect of a transcendent economic logic. One of the more curious aspects of modern times relates to how market institutions facilitate these two entirely opposed ways of talking about the market on the one hand and "the market" on the other.

THE THINGIFICATION OF "THE MARKET"

"A *market* is a shorthand expression for the process by which households' decisions about consumption of alternative goods, firms' decisions about what and how to produce, and workers' decisions about how much and for whom to work are all reconciled by adjustment of *prices*."

David Begg, Stanley Fischer and Rudiger Dornbusch, *Economics*

"Litmus test: If you can't describe Ricardo's Law of Comparative Advantage and explain why people find it counterintuitive, you don't know enough about economics to direct any criticism or praise at 'capitalism' because you don't know what other people are referring to when they use that word."

Eliezer Yudkowsky, co-founder,
Machine Intelligence Research Institute

Inelegant though the phrase certainly is, this book focuses on the process of thingification, of how we get from the abstract account of an economic utopia to a directive political discourse that justifies, and perhaps even mandates, the existence of multiple economic harms. Perhaps more straightforwardly, this might also be thought of as the move from the market concept understood theoretically (and written without the need for the inverted commas) to "the market" understood ideologically (and this time with the inverted commas). The following chapters are written in an attempt to bring greater clarity to the relationship between the market concept as popularized in the abstractions of economic theory and the way in which discussions of how best to govern the economy have increasingly come to revolve around "the market" as a thing. It can be a matter of potential confusion that we have only one word to describe both the market as a conceptual abstraction and "the market" as a political thing. The two meanings are distinct and refer to entirely different aspects of the social world, but in hearing the one word in isolation it is not immediately obvious which of these two meanings is the intended usage. It is not as if you can hear the inverted commas through which I differentiate the market as a concept from "the market" as a thing. The rest of the book will hopefully provide a guide for how to spot the difference between the two and how to challenge any instance in which they are being conflated.

This is not the sort of analysis that it would be usual to find within teaching texts in economics, because they tend only to be interested in the market concept (e.g., Mankiw 2016: 65–88). However, it would be a mistake to therefore assume that their contents have no influence on how "the market" has come to be spoken about as if it has a bodily presence from which it can voice its own opinions about optimal policy settings. This is because the market concept conventionally works within economic theory today to show how individual decisions of what to produce and what to consume can become a functioning economic system. The market concept thus calls to mind the image of a coordinating mechanism that can bring about overall systemic coherence without the need to plan that coordination into existence. From here it does not seem to be too large a step to say that "the market" has both an interest of its own and the will to ensure that its interest is increasingly widely respected. The market concept speaks to the idea that a mechanism exists that can create social order out of what might otherwise be the disorderly context of everybody going about their daily economic business in their own way. Presumably most people would admit to preferring order over disorder, at least with other things being equal, which is one of the everyday sources of political deference to the thing called "the market".

Whilst outwardly there may be no great discursive leap in moving from the market concept to "the market" as a thing, it remains crucial to keep the two separate. The market concept has experienced significant refinement over the years at the hands of economists (Blaug 1996; Backhouse 2002). What was accepted as the meaning of that concept at the birth of modern economics in the late eighteenth century could hardly be more different to the theoretical work that the concept performs in economics today. The difference is so profound that the issue raises its head again of having only one word with many competing meanings (see Chapters 3, 4 and 5). None of these strictly conceptual meanings, however, sustains the image of "the market" as a bodily presence that is capable of ensuring that its interest is successfully acted upon. This is because the market concept operates on a completely different plane of social reality to market ideology. It is an aspect of a purely hypothetical realm in which there are no distributional struggles over economic resources because everyone enjoys formal equality. This realm is created solely to allow for the construction and the clarification of purely theoretical models (Niehans 1994; Morgan 2012). Market ideology, by contrast, relates to actual situations in which all economic resources are fought over, sometimes extremely violently, because the advantage that one person enjoys is an exclusive right that cannot be shared amongst everyone. This is the much messier realm of reality that lacks the clear-cut nature of purely theoretical relationships.

My aim in the following chapters is to enforce a direct engagement between the market concept and the ideology that is carried by the political rhetoric of "the market". At all times I wish to keep the development of economic theory at the forefront of the analysis. The privileges that result today from being able to talk as an economist mean that people's familiarity with economic theory is an important element of the authority that they might acquire as a commentator on public affairs (Turpin 2011). Economic theory thus remains significant to the content of both the market concept and the way in which attempts are made to translate that concept into a political course of action. Yet there will be surprises along the way as the analysis moves sequentially from one chapter to the next. It will become abundantly clear that there is no obvious relationship that can be discerned between the market concept and market ideology, despite the fact that it would appear to be wholly counter-intuitive to presume that the two are completely unconnected.

Many of the most sophisticated refinements of the market concept within economic theory have actually concluded that there should be definite restrictions on the role of market institutions within society (Ingrao & Israel 1990). They have sought to describe the self-made abstract world of a pure market system, but they have done so to show how unrealistic such a system remains as a template for economic relationships that we could ever actually experience. Use of the market concept does not therefore necessarily correlate with the political argument to free "the market" and to defer to its decision-making capacities (Bockman 2011). Even entirely mathematical treatments of the hypothetical realm of voluntarily contracted exchange have concluded that, at a lower level of abstraction, politics will always be necessary to determine where the line should be drawn beyond which market ideology should not be allowed to encroach. Economic theory, then, is not necessarily the proximate source of the jump between the basic market concept and the process of thingification that ends with the argument that governments should always defer to what "the market" says it wants. The history of the market concept might well be glossed over in teaching texts in economics in a way that allows it to be mistaken for an unqualified support prop for market ideology. However, just as with everyone else, there are economists on both sides of the argument about how the economy should be run, and economic theory is therefore far from a homogeneous entity when it comes to reading off political implications. The market concept and market ideology therefore do remain necessarily distinct.

THE DETHINGIFICATION OF "THE MARKET"

"The public has been sold a bill of goods about the free market being a panacea for mankind."

Tom Scholz, rock star and philanthropist

"The market controls everything, but the market has no heart."

Anita Roddick, entrepreneur, human rights activist and
environmental campaigner

If "thingification" is not a word that we are likely to come across often, then "**dethingification**" looks like one that I might just have made up on the spot. Hopefully it will be clear from what has gone before what I mean by this, even if there is a good chance that the word itself is never encountered again. If "the market" has increasingly been turned into a thing in the way that it is invoked politically on all sides of the aisle, how might that process now be reversed so it is no longer spoken about in such a way? What alternative language games might be available, in which it no longer becomes possible to ascribe to market institutions the ability to identify their own interests and the will to act upon them?

The first step in this regard is to reinstate the actual decision-makers who go missing from the analysis when decision-making is instead said to rest with "the market" itself. This is an attribution that occurs almost as a matter of course today, but at the same time it should always be insisted that it is a false attribution. Agency certainly takes place in economic contexts that are bounded by market institutions, and such agency will always be deeply political in its underlying orientation. However, the agent involved is most definitely not "the market" itself. To genuinely perform agency it is first necessary to be aware of what you are attempting to do and to have devised a plan that will hopefully make your chosen ends achievable. It therefore requires a degree of self-consciousness that is not forthcoming for anything other than a fully sensate being. Despite the political language of "the market" now so often portraying it in actor-like terms, it has to be said time and again that market institutions are not actors in their own right. They do not have the requisite emotive and cognitive states to function in the same way in which we would expect humans to ordinarily function.

Despite this, financial market analysts, for instance, now routinely pop up all over the media to give their opinion when they are asked about prevailing "market sentiment" (Peterson 2016). This is shorthand for saying how they expect financial prices to change following an economic event. As one example, the event might be an announcement from the central bank about a change in interest rates, in which case analysts are likely to be responding to questions about what they think will now happen to the structure of prices on the stock market and, from there, to the wealth that people have invested in **mutual funds** tied to the performance of that market. As another example, the event might be an announcement from the finance ministry about a change in the country's debt position, in which case analysts are likely to be responding to questions about what they think will now happen to the structure of prices on the bond market and, from there, to the ability of the government to continue meeting its interest repayments on existing sovereign debts. Governments are today very sensitive to always trying to make sure that financial prices move in the direction that they are hoping for. As such, they expend lots of political energy trying to massage the "mood of the market" in their favour and to gain the analysts' endorsement that "market sentiment" is on their side (Hindmoor 2017).

In truth, of course, there is no such thing as the "mood of the market" or "market sentiment", because market institutions are not the type of sensate beings that can be expected to act in accordance with whether they are in good or bad humour. Yet still we see on almost a routine basis references to the need to assuage market opinion, to satisfy its demands, to attenuate its effects. It is as if market institutions are just waiting to unleash a temper that they find difficult to control, and thus everything that can be done to keep them happy should be done. Politicians might therefore be expected to "take the temperature" of markets at a very early stage of the policy formulation process, before rowing back on their plans at the first sign of its displeasure. In modern politics, then, gaining the good favour and hence the trust of "the market" is just as important as gaining the good favour and hence the trust of the electorate. Whilst no political party is able to get into a position to govern at all if it cannot secure the consent of the electorate, it is a Pyrrhic victory to win an election but not to be able to govern as you wish due to a backlash from "the market". And this tends to be the image with which we are today presented: "the market" as a veto player within the political arena.

This is how the story of the Mitterrand U-turn and the Asian financial crisis are so often told in the existing academic literature. These events are set up as a clash of wills that the politicians were ultimately destined to lose because they had underestimated the veto power of "the market". Mitterrand's good standing in the eyes of the French electorate did not matter in this regard; neither did the track record of successive governments of Thailand, the Philippines, Malaysia, Indonesia and South Korea in delivering headline-grabbing growth figures and accordingly moving many millions of people out of poverty. The only thing that mattered was who had the ability to put everyone else in their place. Here the academic literature tends to come to a very clear conclusion: the wishes of "the market" win out every time over the wishes of governments and their electorates. Even in the case of Bear Stearns the situation is only slightly more complicated. It might have been on the right side of "market sentiment" as it consistently scored very highly during the last five years of its life in *Fortune Magazine*'s prestigious rankings of America's Most Admired Companies (Farlow 2013: 98). Yet, as soon as it found itself on the wrong side, the corrective unleashed by "the market" was both swift and decisive. It will always be thus with an insuperable veto power.

The most interesting feature of this construction of ultimate authority is without doubt how it masks the actual enactment of agency by apportioning it instead to the non-agent of "the market". Politicians routinely point to their inability to withstand the pressure of prevailing market trends. However, whilst it is true that adverse price movements can knock them off course it is also the case that they are not merely passive bystanders being forced to watch helplessly as market logic unfolds to its predetermined end. The pricing structure of all economic markets is set within a legal framework that divides permissible from impermissible actions and, ultimately, the legal framework reflects decisions that have previously been taken at the political level (A. Baker 2014). It might very well appear at times today that market institutions are self-regulating entities where the price level is beyond the influence of elected officials. Yet this follows the decisions that politicians have made to let it look as if it is so. Politicians have themselves been responsible for focusing attention on the inefficiencies of the alleged "big government" phenomenon and for ensuring that the political content of that focus has eroded public trust in decision-making bodies that exist beyond market institutions. If power looks as though it has seeped away from governments and is now located instead in "the market", the oft-encountered spectacle of politicians decrying their ability to act as effective economic regulators helps to explain why.

POLITICIANS TALKING THEMSELVES DOWN

> "This is the permanent tension that lies at the heart of a capitalist democracy and is exacerbated in times of crisis. In order to ensure the survival of the richest, it is democracy that has to be heavily regulated rather than capitalism."
>
> Tariq Ali, radical public intellectual

> "We all too often have socialism for the rich and rugged free market capitalism for the poor."
>
> Martin Luther King, civil rights activist

There are two stand-out reasons for what, on the face of it, might well be the perverse result of politicians talking themselves down. One is a matter of ideology, the other of governing practice. For the first we need to look at the way in which broad approaches to the issue of regulating the economy come in and out of political fashion over time. If we view the post-Second World War period as a whole, there appear to be two distinct trends. These would not have been manifested in every country in exactly the same way at exactly the same time, because each country has its own political institutions whose separate histories would have led them to mediate the dominant trend in their own context-specific ways. Nonetheless, it is still legitimate to think in terms of a dominant trend and to try to characterize it relative to its position on how much "the market" should be allowed to dictate to politicians.

In the early postwar period it was an indication of being in touch with the accepted political wisdom of the time to be vocal in opposing the ever greater encroachment of market ideology (Blyth 2002). There were distinct elements of everyday economic affairs, and of social life more generally, into which market institutions were not allowed to intrude. This was the so-called era of **Keynesianism**, in which governments would routinely overrule pure pricing signals to ensure that there was sufficient demand in the economy to lead to the full utilization of all available resources (Keynes 1937, 1996 [1936]; see also L. Klein 1968; Stewart 1972; Hall 1989; Pasinetti & Schefold 1999; Tily 2007; Steil 2013). For the last forty years, however, the accepted political wisdom has spoken with a very different voice. Where previously it had envisioned a restricted realm for the operation of market ideology, now all currently operative restrictions would seem to be up for grabs (Kiely 2017). Deference to the supposed opinions of "the market" and the construction of "the market" as a legitimate veto player are just two manifestations of the new political common sense. This is the so-called era of **neoliberalism**, in which pure pricing signals are believed to be much better than government intervention at steering the economy towards the desired destination (see Hutton 2001; Amadae 2003; Harvey 2005; Saad-Filho & Johnston 2005; W. Brown 2015; Eagleton-Pierce 2016; Leshem 2016).

However, the increasing use of the political idea of "the market" as a determining political essence is not merely a matter of ideology. It might just as well be a matter of governing practice. Politicians of very many stripes have recently developed an array of tactics through which they can externalize responsibility for policy decisions (Craft & Howlett 2017). This is especially the case when those policies are likely to lead to outcomes that will prove unpopular. If politicians can successfully sustain the image that, even as elected officials, they were not directly responsible for introducing a particular measure, then they hope that they can avoid blame if the repercussions of that measure impact negatively on society as a whole. One example of this is the use of international institutions to enforce policies that ministers might well privately support but do not necessarily want to be associated with publicly (Daugberg & Swinbank 2009). Multilateral agreements that have pushed the globalization agenda in both trade and investment have often accelerated the trend towards deindustrialization that has led to the replacement of stable employment prospects with something noticeably less secure (Standing 2016). No government is going to want to be caught with its fingerprints all over effects of this nature. Instead, they can be expected to activate an externalization strategy. Indeed, in this instance it will tend to be a double externalization strategy.

The first element is likely to involve emphasizing how international law supersedes domestic law and, therefore, having been committed to continued membership of an international institution by the decisions of previous administrations, the government of the day is powerless to plot an independent course. The second element is likely to involve emphasizing that the international institution is, in any case, only embedding the logic of economic globalization. This is where appeals to "the market" come in once again. The logic of economic globalization is typically presented merely as the logic of "the market" scaled up to the world as a whole. There is now a lot of attention in the relevant academic literature on how **depoliticization** strategies like this work. Depoliticization is a process through which the claim is made that the policy is no longer susceptible to the rigours of democratic political debate, because there is an automatic pilot in operation that can produce the policy solution more effectively than the constant give-and-take of politics can ever hope to do (Burnham 2001). Political appeals to the bodily presence and the essential will of "the market" fit the depoliticization template perfectly. The resulting policy will be no less political in terms of the effect it has on life chances if it is explained away as a simple reflection of what "the market" currently wants, but the process through which it was made will allow it to appear as if the politics has been eliminated (Flinders & Buller 2006).

As such, it would seem that the first move that would need to be made to dethingify "the market" in practice would be for politicians to no longer want to thingify it. This in turn would require two steps, each of which represents a significant hurdle in its own right and, taken together, they demonstrate just what a big move is entailed starting where we do today. One is that it would be necessary for politicians to renounce market ideology, but even the global financial crisis has left barely a scratch on its dominance (Crouch 2011; Watson 2014). The other is that politicians would need to forgo the means through which unpopular economic policies do not necessarily translate directly into government unpopularity. There is more than enough in these two factors to demonstrate the immensely solid foundations on which market ideology and, more broadly, the language of "the market" currently reside. Some commentators have recently gone as far as to describe it as an impregnable fortress.

It should nonetheless still go without saying, of course, that the prevailing political common sense is only ever one decisive intervention away from being yesterday's news. Nothing political is ever so set in stone that it becomes fundamentally unchangeable. Yet it remains true that the ideological winds have now been blowing in the same direction for so long that it would be unrealistic to expect "the market" in its current usage to disappear from the political lexicon anytime soon. Dethingification of "the market" does not appear to be anywhere near on the horizon. As such, it makes sense to explore the market concept in greater depth. This will make it possible to learn more about it in its own terms and also what it is about the structure of each variant of the market concept that has allowed its elision with the idea that "the market" exists in a thing-like state and can think and act for itself. The following chapters take up such a challenge.

THE STRUCTURE OF THE BOOK

The remainder of the book comprises five main chapters plus a Conclusion. The political use of the idea of "the market" is never far from the surface of the commentary as I explain how the market concept has evolved over time in the history of economic thought. The presence or absence of inverted commas will therefore continue to matter to what, exactly, it is that is being discussed: whether it is the market concept or "the market" as something that is capable of imposing its own ideological blueprint. The primary focus of the next four chapters is the market concept itself. The following chapter, Chapter 2, will provide an introduction to the three major market concepts that have left an indelible mark on economic theory at various points in its development. Chapters 3, 4 and 5 then provide more detail about each of these market concepts in turn, concentrating in particular on the intellectual context in economics out of which each of them arose. I will be especially keen to emphasize the type of political talk that is facilitated by these three images of the market concept. This will enable me to continue to draw out the difference between the market concept and "the market" as a form of political speech.

Chapter 3 presents the Market Concept Mk 1. This is the market concept that set the tone for the earliest discussion of market institutions in the modern economics tradition. It first came to prominence in the mid-to-late eighteenth century and was the dominant account of the market concept for the best part of the next one hundred years. This was a descriptive market concept that was introduced using words alone and lacked an obvious accompanying mathematical structure. Indeed, the main reason why it was subsequently supplanted was that it became increasingly misaligned with the desire to express basic economic relationships using mathematical logic. It was the market concept pretty much literally as an account of what happens between the counterparties in actually existing marketplaces. The demands it placed on the economist were related more to collecting observable data than to abstract theoretical reflection.

Chapter 4 presents the Market Concept Mk 2. This is the market concept that first allowed economists to say that they were doing more than merely describing extant economic conditions. Instead, they now claimed that they were attempting to capture the essential features of all economic behaviour. They did so through the introduction of the classic demand-and-supply diagram that continues to underpin how the foundations of economic theory are taught today. This is an analytical rather than a descriptive market concept, encouraging economists to think that their primary task was abstract theoretical reflection rather than collecting observable data, and it was used to embed an obvious mathematical logic into basic economic theory for the first time. It was initially seen in the middle of the nineteenth century, but it took a couple of generations from then to really become the dominant approach to the market concept. This dominance lasted unrivalled until the middle of the twentieth century, and this is still the market concept that economics students are most rigorously schooled in today.

Chapter 5 presents the Market Concept Mk 3. Whereas the shift from the Mk 1 to the Mk 2 phase was one of almost complete replacement, there is no similar sense in which the Market Concept Mk 3 supplanted the Mk 2 version. They continue to exist side-by-side, but with the Mk 3 version largely reserved for real theoretical specialists in the field. It remains couched in an analytical as opposed to a descriptive register, but it is constructed using formalist methodology. Its limited take-up can be explained by the significant mathematical demands it places on the economist and the fact that not everyone is willing to commit themselves methodologically to **formalism**. The Market Concept Mk 3 produces the image not of a single market visualized using rudimentary mathematics, so much as an entire market system visualized using extremely sophisticated mathematics. This style of analysis was pioneered in the middle of the twentieth century, and within a generation most of its path-breaking theorems had been published. It remains today only for the theoretical connoisseur of mathematical economics.

Having outlined in turn what I will call the "descriptive", "analytical" and "formalist" market concepts, Chapter 6 and the Conclusion return the analysis more specifically to the language that is used to talk politically about "the market" today. I highlight the fact that it is always a jump to get from the market concept to "the market" understood as a living and breathing thing embodying its own ideological preferences. However, it is still well worthwhile undertaking this sort of analysis because it allows two important subsidiary questions to be asked: what sort of a jump is required, and how large a leap of faith is entailed to get from one to the other? Each of the three variants of the market concept points its own way to how it might be used politically, but none of them offers a straightforward translation into the market ideology that is so familiar today because of its seemingly constant repetition. This once again helps me to reinforce the primary message of the book: namely, the importance of treating the market concept independently of the political discourse of "the market". This is not entirely straightforward to do, as it is the same word in use in both contexts. The complexity entailed in separating out the two always requires extra thought and additional attention to detail, but it can be analytically rewarding if it opens up new perspectives on the central idea through which so much of modern life is governed.

CHAPTER 2

THE MARKET CONCEPT IN TRIPLICATE

INTRODUCTION

"Adam Smith, who has strong claim to being both the Adam and the Smith of systematic economics, was a professor of moral philosophy and it was at that forge that economics was made."

Kenneth Boulding, twentieth-century economic polymath

"[W]e can give an optimistic answer to the logical purist who asks the embarrassing question: "Your economic system isn't determinate until you have found conditions to determine a price *and* a quantity for *each* output and for each input. Do you have enough simultaneous conditions (or equations) to make your interdependent equilibrium system determinate?"

Fortunately, we can answer: "We do have for each output or input *both a supply and a demand condition.* So we can hope that the system will by trial and error in the market place finally settle down – if left undisturbed! – to a determinate competitive equilibrium."

... [E]ven in Adam Smith you can find the germ of the idea if you look hard enough."

Paul Samuelson, *Economics*

In general, the development of the market concept within economic theory has been from the less to the more abstract, and as we move through different levels of abstraction we should probably expect to encounter entirely different types of market concept. Not that this is revealed in the economics textbooks too often. They tend instead to present students with only one market model, that based on neoclassical **demand-and-supply dynamics**. It is conventionally known as the **partial equilibrium** model to denote the way in which it depicts how the pricing structure might balance demand and supply in one market alone at one moment in time. Sometimes the textbooks will use this as a precursor to introducing the **general equilibrium** model, a much more abstract model that explains the conditions that would have to be in place for demand and supply to be brought into perfect harmony in every conceivable market at all moments in time. But this is by no means the norm.

It is only on occasions, then, that there is some attempt to show what came after the neoclassical demand-and-supply model in the long march towards the highest imaginable level of abstraction. However, this is typically not mirrored in attempts to show what preceded it. Teaching texts in economics tend not to explore the history of economic thought, treating it as an unnecessary diversion from the primary objective of what the market concept is taken to mean in the here and now. Yet if we want to know more about what the textbooks do want us to learn as the market concept, then presumably we should also want to enquire into what they do *not*. Much is revealed in general about accepted conceptual meanings by studying alternative meanings that are now usually suppressed.

As is so often the case in economics, the story of the first market concept should probably begin with Adam Smith and his *Wealth of Nations*, even if his market concept was merely building upon that of his predecessors (Aspromourgos 1996). The textbooks will usually nod deferentially in Smith's direction and pay due reverence to his ostensible status as "father" of the discipline. But students are typically not directed towards examining his books in their original detail. Smith's own work is considered to be too dated for today's students to spend their time on (Peil 2000). Perhaps it contained flashes of intuition that later economists were able to flesh out into general economic principles, we are told, but Smith himself is widely considered to have not been up to that task, despite all of his subsequent fame. If economics is about what economists believe to be true theoretically today, this argument goes, then there is no need to start rooting around in eighteenth-century treatises, because that is not the place to find them.

The two most important textbook writers of the post-Second World War heyday of **neoclassical economics** made their opinions very clear in this regard. Each was subsequently awarded the Nobel Memorial Prize in Economic Sciences, and therefore their standing as theorists is every bit as elevated as their standing as textbook writers. However, when it comes to the specific issue of the market concept, they have been responsible for closing the discussion down rather than opening it up in the manner that we might expect of theoretical pioneers. Their work has provided their economist colleagues with a much narrower view of the market concept than would otherwise likely have been the case.

George Stigler, the author of *The Theory of Price*, the 1946 textbook that ran to four editions and was originally called *The Theory of Competitive Price*, was the more dismissive of the two (G. Stigler 1946). His view on the significance for economists of knowing the origins of their subject field is best summed up by his observation that: "The economics of 1800, like the weather forecasts of 1800, is mostly out of date" (G. Stigler 1969: 218). For Stigler, what counts for economics students is so much what economists believe to be true theoretically today that if there is no obviously direct theoretical link between past and present then the past can be safely forgotten. Neoclassical economics does indeed mark a clear break with Smith's concept of the market, as it would be extremely hard to identify any sense of pre-emption in operation here (Winch 1997). Only by wilfully crowbarring the text of *The Wealth of Nations* into a decidedly more modern template can such a link be drawn. It is therefore difficult to escape the conclusion that, from Stigler's perspective at least, it is entirely justifiable to simply bypass what Smith had in mind when his attention turned to the meaning of the market concept.

Paul Samuelson, the author of the 1948 textbook *Economics*, which ran to nineteen editions, was a little more conciliatory in his approach to the history of economic thought (Samuelson 1948a). Yet even here we must take care to note that the rapprochement he sought between older and newer forms of economic theory was to take place very much on the territory of the latter. "Inside every classical writer", he argued, "there is a modern economist trying to get born" (Samuelson 1992: 5). Smith's market concept could be seen as a pre-emption of what came later from Samuelson's perspective, but only if that later theory could be used as a corrective to what was obviously missing from the original account (Boulding 1971). Samuelson made his name by bringing a new mathematical approach to the basic building blocks of economic theory, thus erecting a formal edifice for all subsequent theoretical endeavours. He was clear in his own mind where Smith had gone wrong. Under his approach, if a mathematical system was to have a solution then it must contain the same number of unknowns in the equations as the number of equations in the system (Samuelson 1983). Samuelson was able to show that, in his terms at least, Smith was working with many more unknowns than his explanation could handle. This, though, was to mistake the purpose of what Smith had been trying to do. He could only have erred in the construction of the mathematical system that Samuelson later imputed to him if he had intended to create such a system in the first place. But this would be a wholesale misattribution of intention. It was Samuelson and not Smith two hundred years before who asked to be judged in this way.

Of the two Nobel Laureates who provided neoclassical economics with textbooks during its postwar heyday, Samuelson was certainly more amenable to an engagement with Smith's text. Yet it was Stigler, dismissive in tone though he was, who was more to the point in insisting that Smith had started off with a fundamentally different notion of what the word "market" was to mean. Later generations of neoclassical economists might well have used the same word within their theories, but what they had in mind when subsequently refining their own market model was almost entirely unrecognisable from within the framework of Smith's concept.

My approach in this book is the exact opposite of that of these path-breaking textbook writers. It is to open up the discussion about the market concept rather than to close it down; it is about restoring the historical account of the origins of various market concepts rather than suppressing it. The historical chapters follow next. In the meantime, the aim of this chapter is to introduce the three competing concepts around which the historical chapters will be organized. Working forwards in time from the oldest, I distinguish, in turn, between a descriptive, an analytical and a formalist market concept, before showing the highly uneven nature of their incorporation into contemporary economics textbooks.

THE MARKET AS A DESCRIPTIVE CONCEPT

> "When the price of any commodity is neither more nor less than what is sufficient to pay the rent of the land, the wages of the labour, and the profits of the stock employed in raising, preparing, and bringing it to market, according to their natural rates, the commodity is then sold for what may be called its natural price … The commodity is then sold precisely for what it is worth."
>
> Adam Smith, *An Inquiry into the Nature and Causes*
> *of the Wealth of Nations*

> "No society can surely be flourishing and happy, of which the far greater part of the members are poor and miserable."
>
> Adam Smith, *An Inquiry into the Nature and Causes of*
> *the Wealth of Nations*

The most notable aspect of Smith's market concept is just how literal it seems to be. We are familiar today with what a market looks like in physical form, and this is probably what first springs to mind when hearing the word. It may well be called different things around the world, from the bazaar of ancient Persia to the souk of Western Asia and North Africa, the agora of ancient Greece and the rialto of pre-renaissance Venice. But the basic physical form is very much the same. It is the aggregation of a number of individual stallholders, who come together in a given place because it is here that they have a legal right to trade. Archaeological studies have dated back this type of economic arrangement around four thousand years (Sanderson 2013). Even the more modern phenomenon of the supermarket or the *hypermarché* does little to corrupt this physical form. It continues to house many types of vendor under one roof, the only real difference being that the whole enterprise is now owned by one company (Humphery 1998).

Smith's references to the market concept in *The Wealth of Nations* are almost all cast in the image of this physical form. When thinking of later accounts of the market concept that emphasize the creation of **equilibrium** through demand-and-supply dynamics, it is clear that this is not a place that we could ever visit. It has no real coordinates because it is purely a product of the mind, an abstraction. There is no sense in which it can ever escape the theorists' self-made abstract world to re-emerge in recognisable form in the real world. The exact opposite is true of Smith's market concept. It refers to something that could not be more real in that it has a physical presence and invokes a place the type of which we can recall visiting many times over.

Even the broader phrase within which the market concept appears in so many of the key theoretical passages in *The Wealth of Nations* calls this underlying materiality instantly to mind. Throughout the famous Chapter VII of Book I, Smith alluded time and again to goods specifically being physically transported to market. In the first half of that chapter alone, there are nine instances where he writes of goods being "brought" to market, six of people "bringing" goods to market and one use each of "brings" and "bring" to convey exactly the same message (Smith 1981 [1776/1784]: I.vii.4–17). This makes it clear that when he referred to the concept it meant somewhere that one could expect to see actual commercial activity taking place in front of one's eyes. This is the market literally as a marketplace, with all the hustle and bustle of people going about their business and trying to secure a livelihood. It is a place of effort as vendors try their hardest to make a sale and it is also a place of noise and emotion as selling strategies are put into practice. It is not the hypothetical realm of later market concepts in which ideal-type economic agents behave passively to act out the equilibrium logic of demand-and-supply dynamics. To differentiate it from what came later, I will call what is to be found in Smith's *Wealth of Nations*, amongst other books of that era, the Market Concept Mk 1 or the descriptive market concept.

Samuelson was mistaken in thinking that Smith's concept of market as marketplace was an early intimation of what a purely mathematical system of market relations might look like. In turn, Stigler was also mistaken in thinking that Smith's concept of market as marketplace was an argument in favour of creating a self-regulating market system for the conduct of all economic activity. At a banquet held in Glasgow in 1976 to commemorate the bicentenary of the first edition of *The Wealth of Nations*, Stigler (cited in Meek 1977: 3) declared that Smith "is alive and well and living in Chicago". This proprietorial claim was not meant to imply that the **Chicago School** of which Stigler was an important member had a carbon copy of Smith's market concept, so much as they had a common vision of a freely negotiated market society and that this should be seen as the ideal. However, he is far from alone in misstating the essence of Smith's interest in the market worldview. There is a persistent suggestion that Smith's studies of eighteenth-century marketplaces translate unequivocally into all-out advocacy of "the market" (McLean 2006). Further reflection is definitely necessary, though, before committing to this point of view.

Taking Smith's philosophical writings in tandem with his economic writings, it becomes much more difficult to sustain the argument that he was attempting to do no more than simply promote the introduction of further market institutions whatever the underlying social question was. In this regard, the Smith that members of the University of Chicago's Economics Department thought was stalking their corridors was a Smith of their making and not his (Medema 2010). The Smith that spoke in his own voice believed that everyday economic life was evolving around him to the point at which the jump might be made into a full-blown commercial society (Rasmussen 2008). His work was designed to explore the role that might be played by market exchange in this new society. Smith's philosophical reflections are to be found in his *Theory of Moral Sentiments*, which was published in 1759, seventeen years before his more famous *Wealth of Nations*. There he asked about the characteristics that the market agent would have to display if the exchange relation was to be structured in a way that avoided being conspicuously disadvantageous to one of its participants.

Smith had a notion of equality that involved the right to be secured from harm (Griswold 1999). This was a radical conception for his day, especially if we consider the terms on which the fledgling factory labour force was being contracted at the time (Thompson 2016 [1963]). *The Wealth of Nations* says very little about the world of work, however, and when Smith investigated the structure of harms within the exchange relation he tended to do so in terms of how trade took place between a buyer and a seller of a physical good rather than the buyer and seller of labour. He was interested primarily in how one presented themselves to the other as they tried to negotiate a fair price for the good that would influence not only this particular transaction but also future possible transactions (Smith 1981 [1776/1784]: I.ii.2). To this end he asked whether the commercial spirit necessarily undermined both transacting parties' commitment to respecting the other's right to avoid harm. When expressed like this, it is fairly straightforward to see why he would want to concentrate his account on those moments in which real commercial activity occurred and why, as a consequence, his market concept would invoke the physical form of actual commercial marketplaces. In addition, it is also fairly straightforward to see why later generations of economists would want to work with a different market concept to Smith's, because their focus was on the essence of fundamentally economic behaviour stripped of all of its social influences, whereas he seems to have been asking an entirely different category of question.

Samuelson's account of Smith's work is different to Stigler's, but it too in its own way misstates it. As with other neoclassical economists, Samuelson placed at the heart of his market concept the practice of price adjustment in the progress towards equilibrium (Negishi 1982). He then appears to have gone looking in *The Wealth of Nations* for the sort of pre-emption of his own later concept that Stigler thought was unlikely ever to be apparent in the work of eighteenth-century theorists. He found it in a single sentence in Chapter Seven of Book I of what, in total, is the 950-page *Wealth of Nations*. Smith was a well-known admirer of the work of Isaac Newton, believing that his 1687 *Philosophiæ Naturalis Principia Mathematica* captured perfectly the one true scientific method. He referred to Newton's "superior genius and sagacity", suggesting that he was responsible for "the greatest and most admirable improvement that was ever made" in the subjects he studied (Smith 1982a: IV.67). Newtonian intimations are never more apparent in the text of *The Wealth of Nations* than in the sentence that seems to have caught Samuelson's eye. It is to be found in the chapter where Smith explained the difference between the "natural price" and "market prices". "The natural price", he wrote, "is, as it were, the central price, to which the prices of all commodities are continually gravitating" (Smith 1981 [1776/1784]: I.vii.15). Samuelson identified in Smith's concept of the natural price his own of the equilibrium price, because within his market model the equilibrium price is indeed the central price. It is the price at which the economic system comes to rest and the mathematical system of equations is solved. Here, demand complements supply in a perfect symmetry between the two sides of the market, and as a consequence the process of price adjustment ceases (Samuelson 1941).

Yet Smith had something very different in mind. By the natural price he meant the price at which both parties would be happy to enter the exchange as either buyer or seller. To the extent that this represents symmetry between the two sides of the market, it is not the quantitative neoclassical symmetry in which there are exactly the right number of buyers to purchase all of the available products that have been put on sale. It is, instead, a symmetry of treatment, where everyone acts in relation to people on the other side of the market how they hope other people would act towards them were the roles to be reversed. In other words, it represents a situation in which all harms have been removed from the act of exchange, because anyone who is attentive to the possibility of role reversal will not want to impose hurt on other people that they might subsequently have to bear themselves. Everyone is consequently able to realize in the physical marketplace neither no more nor no less than what they believe they are selling is worth, whether that product is something that they have made with their labour or whether it is their labour itself. Smith made it clear that there can be no presumption when using his market concept, unlike when using the market concept of the neoclassical economists, that the natural price will prevail.

THE MARKET AS AN ANALYTICAL CONCEPT

> "'Perfect competition' is considered both the ideal and the default state in Economics 101. So-called perfectly competitive markets achieve equilibrium when producer supply meets consumer demand."
>
> Peter Thiel, businessman and economic commentator

> "You can make even a parrot into a learned political economist. All he must learn are the two words 'supply' and 'demand'."
>
> Probably apocryphal, but typically attributed to the philosopher Thomas Carlyle

The foregoing acts as a reminder of how these first two market concepts operate at very different levels of abstraction. Smith's descriptive market concept belongs within the real world of livelihood struggles being played out against the backdrop of power asymmetries. He was adamant that within such a world there could be no assurance that market prices would ever come to settle at the level of the natural price (Smith 1981 [1776/1784]: I.iv.17). The neoclassical market concept, which I treat as an analytical market concept, assumes that the process of price adjustment will always come to a pre-ordained resting place consistent with the practice of voluntarily contracted exchange (Tieben 2012). This is because it exists solely in the hypothetical realm of economic theory, where the assumption of wantonly idealized circumstances is not necessarily a problem. By contrast, Smith's analysis in *The Wealth of Nations* is shot through with much more practical concerns (Winch 1978). It is difficult to read the book as a whole and not come to the conclusion that he was worried that market prices might always be at a level higher than the natural price when products are on sale and at a level lower than the natural price when labour is on sale. Smith (1981 [1776/1784]: I.vii.15) wrote rather obliquely about the influence of "[d]ifferent accidents" that enforce these disparities. Some vested interest will always be in play, he argued, to frustrate the manifestation of the natural price. This helps to highlight the distinctiveness of Smith's market concept (which recognizes the fact that market institutions always reflect the prevailing political balance of power) when viewed through the perspective of the market concepts that followed it (which do not).

By removing the distorting influence of the self-interested exercise of power, the analytical market concept of neoclassical economics was designed to investigate abstract **market-clearing dynamics**. A market can be said to have cleared when every buyer has access to sufficient stocks of the product to satisfy their optimal consumption plan and every seller exhausts their previously unsold inventory of stocks (Barro 2008). This would be such a demanding criterion in the real world that we can be sure that it belongs solely to the theorists' world of hypothetical economic relationships. Allowing for that restriction, it suggests that the prevailing price level is as right as it can ever be. If it was even a fraction higher than the equilibrium price a number of people would regard the product as either unaffordable or, at the very least, not worth the money that was being charged for it. In either case they would remove it from their optimal consumption plan and thereby ensure that some stocks would remain unbought. Conversely, if the prevailing price level was even a fraction lower than that required for equilibrium, then this would mean that a number of producers would be unable to cover their costs. They might be able to take out a bank loan to temporarily tide themselves over, but this could never be more than a short-term expedient. At least some producers would eventually have to cease supplying the market, at which point many consumers would find that there were no longer enough products on sale to optimize their consumption plans.

Hopefully the significance of the equilibrium condition to the Market Concept Mk 2 should become immediately apparent. Equilibrium is the only situation in which a market will clear. In every one of the infinite situations of disequilibrium there will be an imbalance that enforces some degree of asymmetry between the two sides of the market. There are four generic sources of disequilibrium – too much demand, too little demand, too much supply, too little supply – and each requires that the process of adjustment continues before the system of equations being described by the analytical market concept might be solved. The equations themselves require that all economic agents are well behaved and act solely on the basis of the cues that they take from price signals (Krugman & Wells 2015). They cannot be motivated by power or greed or even the wish to retire one day significantly wealthier than the life they were born into. There can be no distractions in trying to get one over someone else, whether that is exploiting tax loopholes, for example, or taking advantage of legislation designed to curb trade union power, or even merely sniffing out a bargain when a product is accidentally under-priced. The Market Concept Mk 2 is thus exceptionally exacting in the behavioural conformity that it requires of its hypothetical agents.

The Market Concept Mk 3 is even more demanding. It is at least relatively straightforward to describe in words what its predecessor requires its hypothetical agents to do. In the formalist market concept, however, they are merely epiphenomenal of a dictating mathematical logic. They therefore have all the clarity that is to be expected of a deterministic mathematical essence. In a bid to ensure that the very possibility of a behavioural exception is removed, the rules that shape economic interaction here are extended to an infinite number of agents operating across an infinite number of markets and an infinite time horizon (Warsh 1993).

THE MARKET AS A FORMALIST CONCEPT

"General equilibrium is the statement that all the different parts of the economy influence each other, even if it's remote, like mortgage-backed securities and their demands on automobiles."

Kenneth Arrow, Nobel laureate for his contribution
to general equilibrium economics

"Mathematical modeling is a mixed blessing for economics. [It] provides real advantages in terms of precision of thought ... But the costs are not zero. Mathematical modeling limits what can be tackled and what is considered legitimate inquiry."

David Kreps, *Microeconomic Foundations I:*
Choice and Competitive Markets

The difference between the market concept in its Mk 2 and Mk 3 phases is defined in theoretical terms as the difference between a partial equilibrium and a general equilibrium system. Within a partial equilibrium system the object of interest is one market for a single product. This does not take into account, however, the way in which executing optimal consumption and production plans in one market can change what count as optimal consumption and production plans in other markets. If two goods are close substitutes, such as a bus ride or a train journey between the same starting point and same destination, the adjustment towards equilibrium in the market for bus tickets will have consequential effects on the relationship between demand and supply in the market for train tickets. Creating conditions of equilibrium in one of these two markets might therefore move the existing state of demand and supply further away from equilibrium in the other market. There are spillover effects, in other words, that need to be taken into account if a more holistic understanding of market-clearing dynamics is to be developed. This is the objective of the move from a partial equilibrium to a general equilibrium frame of reference. Within such a framework, the object of interest is the market system as a whole. The mathematics underpinning this way of thinking allows for that system to be comprised of every market for every product that might be imagined both now and in the future.

The shift between the Market Concept Mks 2 and 3 is thus, more than anything, a shift between one set of mathematical techniques that underpins an avowedly analytical market concept and another that facilitates the development of an explicitly formalist market concept. It is consistent with ever greater demands being placed on the mathematical training of the economic theorist. Samuelson, remember, had called Smith to task for working with a theoretical model that was very difficult to render intelligible in mathematical terms. The major shortcoming of his theory, from Samuelson's (1992) perspective at least, was that it was impossible to derive enough equations from it to match the number of unknowns within it. The problem of too many unknowns therefore posed difficulties when it came to positing a system of simultaneous equations that might successfully mathematize the market concept. The **marginalist** pioneers of the late nineteenth century were first able to show what a system of this nature might look like (Sandmo 2011), but they had to engineer a complete break with Smith's market concept to do so. Samuelson worked with a much more sophisticated set of mathematical tools in the 1940s, operating within the same broad field of algebra as contained the marginalists' simultaneous equations, but incorporating a new technique in which inequalities took the place of equalities in the equations (Weintraub 1991). But even this began to look very old-fashioned very quickly as a new generation of general equilibrium theorists started to remodel the market concept on the basis of combining the most cutting-edge developments in topology and convex set theory (Urai 2010).

Despite the embrace of increasingly sophisticated mathematical techniques the difference between the analytical and formalist market concepts is less pronounced than that between either and the descriptive market concept. Equilibrium provides the analytical and formalist market concepts with a common conceptual core, with both focusing as a consequence on market-clearing dynamics. The one big conceptual change across the two relates to the scope of application of the equilibrium situation. I have already argued that its application in partial equilibrium terms places demands on the market concept that undermine any easy association with conditions that might be experienced in the real world. To bring demand and supply into alignment for just one market in a single product is a sufficiently exacting standard in its own right. Imagine, then, what it would take for the same alignment to arise for every conceivable market in every conceivable product across an indefinite time horizon. This is the standard that the successful solution of a general equilibrium system requires. It is possible to derive such a solution mathematically, but we should not mistake this for a genuinely economic solution (Watson 2005b).

General equilibrium models speak to markets for every product that has yet to be invented but will be at some stage in the future. They also speak to markets for every type of exchange that has yet to be legalized but will be at some stage in the future. Their coverage is thus spectacular in its breadth. Only the generality that can be captured by the reach into infinity of convex set theory is capable of delivering such unprecedented scope. The human mind is able to specify such far-reaching mathematical models, but it is beyond human cognitive capacities to name in economic terms every market that is thereby entailed. The Market Concept Mk 3 exists as a logical possibility within theorists' self-made abstract world, but only in that form. Nobody can relive their everyday economic experiences and imagine themselves in the context captured by the formalist market concept in the same way that they can in the context captured by the descriptive market concept. General equilibrium models have a curious dual characteristic of being irreducibly products of the mind but simultaneously impossible to call to mind in any familiarly recognisable form.

THE MARKET CONCEPT IN THE ECONOMICS TEXTBOOKS

> "Economists normally presume that the price of a good or a service moves quickly to bring quantity supplied and quantity demanded into balance. In other words, they assume that markets are normally in equilibrium, so the price of any good or service is found where the supply and demand curves intersect. This assumption is called market clearing."
>
> Gregory Mankiw and Mark Taylor, *Macroeconomics*

> "Economics puts parameters on people's utopias, and the teachings of the principles of economics should inform as much on what *not* to do, perhaps even more than providing a guide to public action."
>
> Peter Boettke, *Living Economics*

Almost without exception, the analytical market concept is what the beginning student is first asked to learn (Begg, Fischer & Dornbusch 2008). They are very quickly socialized via teaching texts into attempting to subject all of the world's problems to its equilibrium solution. This, they are told, is the imprint of having come to know how to think like an economist (Mankiw 2016: 19–46). The demand-and-supply model provides economics students with the language that will guide them successfully through their degree programmes and, even more profoundly, it also provides them with their subsequent professional instincts. It is a source of significant rhetorical power, both within economics and beyond, and that rhetorical power can relatively easily be cashed in for social authority (McCloskey 1998). Being able to comment specifically as an economist is a favoured form of expertise in the modern world, but this first requires not only familiarity with the analytical market concept but also a willingness to believe that even the most straightforward demand-and-supply model produces valuable insights into

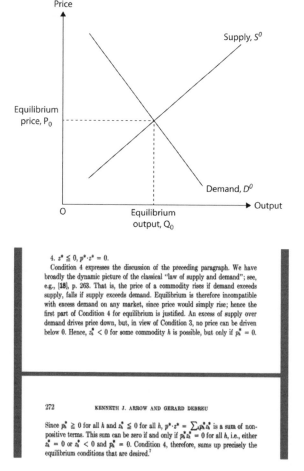

Figure 2.1: The classic demand-and-supply diagram and part of the mathematical proof of the existence conditions for general equilibrium

all aspects of social living. Whatever it is that one wants to talk about must be retrofitted into a market model that contains a demand curve, a supply curve and a point of equilibrium.

Given this, it is perhaps understandable that the economics textbooks often present the formalist market concept as a mere extension of the analytical market concept. If it is the Mk 2 phase that really does provide economists with the instincts that make them the experts of everything, then it is not to be expected that the textbooks will admit that there is something else available that goes beyond it in a qualitative sense (Fine 2004). Subsequent chapters, however, will be used to demonstrate that there are actually some very significant differences between the two. The first thing to note in this regard is just how different they look. On the top on the previous page is the classic **demand-and-supply diagram** that captures the most common depiction of the market concept as a distinctly analytical phenomenon, whilst on the bottom is an excerpt from the classic account of the market concept as a distinctly formalist phenomenon (Arrow & Debreu 1954: 271–2). Both rely on mathematical logic, and in this way they share a stance in clear distinction to the descriptive treatment of the market concept as a physical marketplace. Yet this is not to say that the two could ever be confused with one another in the most basic feel that they deliver to the reader.

The mathematical treatment of the market concept in its Mk 2 phase remains somewhat hidden behind the analytical façade, at least to the extent to which the mathematical logic is only ever implicit in its dominant visual representation. This takes the form of a diagram that will be instantly recognisable to anyone who has ever enrolled on a formal course in economics. It is comprised of a y-axis going vertically up the page that denotes price, and an x-axis going horizontally along the page that denotes output. Onto this two-dimensional space demand and supply curves, D^o and S^o, are drawn for the particular market under consideration. They are conventionally called "curves" in any case, even though they are equally conventionally depicted today as straight lines. The demand curve is downward sloping from top left to bottom right of the two-dimensional space. The underlying assumption here is that every incremental reduction in the product's asking price will reveal progressively more people who would be willing to pay that price to take the product into their possession. Thus the price reduction can be thought to bring more people into the market on its demand side. Meanwhile, the supply curve is upward sloping from bottom left to top right of the two-dimensional space. This captures the assumption that it is necessary for the market price to rise, rather than fall, if more people are to be brought into the market on its supply side. At the lowest possible conceivable price only the producer with the lowest costs of production will be able to supply the market. But every incremental price rise will allow increasingly inefficient producers to cover their basic costs of production. There is a single point at which the two curves cross, and this is the point at which the market can be said to be in equilibrium, with an equilibrium price P_o and equilibrium output Q_o. Here it clears perfectly, because there are exactly the right number of production units being supplied to the market to match demand in its entirety.

This, then, is the partial equilibrium model of the interaction between demand and supply in the market for a single product. It remains necessarily mathematical because the equilibrium solution to the model is, in fact, the mathematical solution to a system of simultaneous equations. But it does not take on that appearance in the economics textbooks. This is because the solution is much easier to grasp as a matter of pure analytical intuition when the model is presented diagrammatically rather than algebraically. The mind's eye has to be trained in a particular way to be able to "see" the solution to a partial equilibrium model when it is presented as a system of simultaneous equations. By contrast, the eye is drawn directly to the point of intersection in a demand-and-supply diagram, and in this sense the solution to a partial equilibrium model is "visible" much more literally. The important point in this regard is that a system of simultaneous equations exists in a two-dimensional mathematical space, and this is relatively easy to transpose into the two-dimensional representational space of the classic demand-and-supply diagram. Perhaps it is no coincidence, as will be shown in the following chapter, that the origins of the diagram predate the first use in economics of **differential calculus** to present the solution to the partial equilibrium model through higher-order algebra.

The same does not typically hold true for the general equilibrium model that provides the basis for the formalist market concept. The reams of mathematical formulae through which the general equilibrium model is constructed in this latter instance are almost always *in themselves* also the visual representation of the concept. There is only a very limited sense of being able to call to mind a simple image of a solution to a general equilibrium model as a single point. The one notable exception in this regard is Francis Ysidro Edgeworth's (2003 [1881]: 28) famous account of a **contract curve**, which was later placed into the "box diagram" that now conventionally bears Edgeworth's name by first Vilfredo Pareto (1971 [1906]: 187) and then Arthur Bowley (1924: 5).

As can be seen from Figure 2.2 below, there are two goods, X and Y, to be distributed between two people, A and B. A's **indifference curves** for X and Y have their point of origin in the bottom-left corner and go outwards towards the top-right corner for every additional combination of X and Y that becomes feasible given the initial allocation of resources between the two people. The reverse is true of B, whose indifference curves go progressively

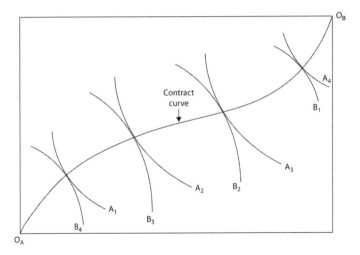

Figure 2.2: The Edgeworth box diagram

outwards from the top-right corner to the bottom-left corner. The further up the diagram away from O_A the greater the proportion of Y that ends up in A's possession, and the further to the right on the diagram away from O_A the greater the proportion of X that ends up in A's possession. B gains in a similar manner the more that the agreed distribution departs from O_B. Agreement arises, said Edgeworth, when there is no possibility of either person gaining from a reallocation of X and Y without the other person having to accept a loss (Starr 1997). All the positions within the box are possible allocations, but Edgeworth suggested that only a small subset of these points represented efficient allocations where all the gains from exchange are exhausted. He drew a line through these points and called them the contract curve, which Pareto and Bowley formalized into the box diagram through the use of indifference curves. They showed that the individual points of the contract curve were themselves points of tangency between the indifference curves of each individual (A_1/B_4, A_2/B_3, A_3/B_2, A_4/B_1, etc.) (Martín-Román 2004).

However, the proponents of general equilibrium economics today show no desire to limit their ambitions to talking about a two-person, two-good world. Even expanding the model to three people and three goods provides a zone of negotiation over the optimal allocation that operates across a sufficiently large number of dimensions to leave it irreducible to a single point that can be summoned easily to the human mind. Yet modern-day general equilibrium theorists would not think that they were worthy of the name if they decided to stop there. Their model world comprises an infinitely large number of people and an infinitely large number of goods. Supercomputers are capable of drawing images of infinite-dimension relationships if they have sufficient processing power. But what emerges is not what we see in our mind's eye when we are asked to envision a single point. It most certainly is not something that resembles an Edgeworth box in any way whatsoever.

For these infinite-dimension relationships that are now the standard fare of general equilibrium economics, the mathematics is not concealed behind a simple two-dimensional diagram but is instead front and centre of the presentation. Maybe this is why the textbooks often invite economics students to think of the general equilibrium model merely as an extension of the partial equilibrium model. It would certainly be comforting to think that there was a commensurable visual feature that could act as the representation of the solution to both these models. This would lie within easy intuitive reach, but unfortunately it is simply disqualified by the mathematical structure of the general equilibrium model and its capacity for reaching into infinity.

Moreover, the mathematics also changes the content of the economics between the analytical market concept of partial equilibrium and the formalist market concept of general equilibrium. This is likely to go completely unremarked upon in the economics textbooks that want to treat the two as being of the same generic kind. The difference is there nonetheless, even though it is often further masked by the rather confusing use of the same economic vocabulary across the two market concepts. We can explore this phenomenon by going back to the classic demand-and-supply diagram and reminding ourselves of what appears on the two axes. Indeed, it is not necessary to be too far into even an introductory economics course before you no longer need a reminder of this nature. As every economics student will know because the answer will have been drummed into them pretty much from day one of their course, it is price on the y-axis and output on the x-axis.

It is the concepts of price and output that provide the classic demand-and-supply diagram with economic meaning insofar as they are quantitatively oriented. In this instance, though, "quantitative" does not mean "enumerated" in any straightforward experimental sense. Nothing is typically counted before the demand and supply curves are drawn onto the two-dimensional space with which we are so familiar. Yet this does not make the underlying concepts of price and output that bring the classic demand-and-supply diagram to life any less quantitative in their basic orientation. The economic logic that the diagram communicates requires anyone who looks at the diagram to know without a moment's hesitation that the further away you go from the diagram's point of origin the greater the quantity being represented by the demand and supply curves.

This can be simply illustrated by looking at the economic conditions that distinguish between two points on the demand curve and the supply curve respectively. In both of these instances, as shown in Figure 2.3, the relevant difference is that between point A and point B. For the demand curve shown, imagine that the underlying conditions in this market are such that there

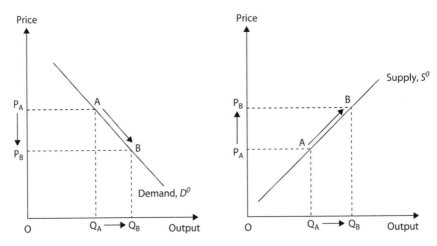

Figure 2.3: Diagrams showing movements along the demand and supply curves

are sufficient consumers in the market at price P_A to demand output Q_A. What would have to change for more consumers to enter the market and for demand to now be consistent with output Q_B? Quite clearly, the market price would have to fall to P_B. All three of these changes – the increased number of consumers, the higher quantity demanded and the lower price – are quantitative in nature. It is likewise in the case of the supply curve. How can we expand the number of firms in the market so that the quantity supplied rises from output Q_A to Q_B? The simple answer is to allow the price to rise from P_A to P_B, which will enable a number of less efficient producers to also enter the market as the higher price provides a backdrop for them to be able to cover their costs.

It was this basic intuition that caused Stanley Jevons to famously declare in the preface to the second edition of his *Theory of Political Economy* that, by definition, economics had to be a mathematical science because every feature of everyday economic life with which it deals is in principle able to be enumerated. "[T]he mathematical treatment of Economics is coeval with the science itself", he stated matter-of-factly (Jevons 2013 [1879]: lxiii). And who could object to this most elemental claim in relation to mathematizing the field? Surely little more than straightforward instinct is required to know that the higher the price the more people there will be who can afford to make the product but the fewer there will be who can afford to buy it. There are quantities involved here, and those quantities can therefore be counted and written in numbers. Even though Jevons was instrumental in effecting the break with Smith's market concept, he thought that the two of them perceived of economic theory in exactly the same way at this most basic of levels, enlisting "the father of the science" as a direct predecessor in expressing his theory in a manner that was "thoroughly mathematical": "we find Adam Smith continually arguing about 'quantities of labour', 'measures of value', 'measures of hardship', 'proportion', 'equality', etc.; the whole of the ideas in fact are mathematical" (Jevons 2013 [1879]: xliii).

Now consider what price and output come to mean within the general equilibrium model. Things get much more complicated in this instance, which no doubt merely reflects the move from one already abstract account of the market concept to a much more abstract alternative. Price and output become merely the names that are given to two of the vectors that appear within the account of myriad market interactions that can be delivered by convex set theory. However, price in this instance is merely the letter combinations "p", "r", "i", "c" and "e", and output the letter combinations "o", "u", "t", "p", "u" again and "t" again. The mathematics of convex set theory works in exactly the same way irrespective of how the vectors of which it is comprised are labelled. Their names are immaterial to whether the mathematics works; it stands or falls on its own terms. These vectors could therefore be called anything that a random letter generator might decide that they are called. The fact that economic theorists have given them economic-sounding names does nothing to ensure that they actually carry any essential economic meaning. At heart this must always be an arbitrary naming strategy.

CONCLUSION

"In a market system, coordination is accomplished in a decentralized fashion by prices."

Michael Katz and Harvey Rosen, *Microeconomics*

"Market clearing is a powerful assumption."

Stanley Fischer and Rudiger Dornbusch, *Macroeconomics*

The market concept is thus by no means a single thing. Different uses of that concept are distinguishable by time, because what it was taken to mean by the first of the modern economists in the eighteenth century has almost no bearing on the way in which their successors deploy it today. However, it is also distinguishable both methodologically and ontologically. Methodologically what is important is not only the way in which it has gone from a non-mathematical to a mathematical concept, but also how very different mathematical goals separate the partial equilibrium model from the general equilibrium model. Ontologically, the shift has been from the less to the more abstract. Whilst making this move, the market concept has been increasingly emptied of the economic content that comes from treating it as a descriptive concept. This might look at first glance to be a rather curious thing to say about the most important concept in the whole of contemporary economics. Yet it remains true in the sense that progressively less effort has to be made as we move through phases one to three of the market concept to verify the relationships it presumes through observational data drawn from everyday economic life.

There is much to gain, therefore, in thinking of the market concept not as a simple undifferentiated entity, so much as through the type of disaggregated account that appears in this chapter. However, this does nothing to make it easier to guard against the tendency for the market concept to be used in everyday forms of speech as if "the market" had a determining will that it was able to impose upon the rest of society. If anything, it complicates matters still further. I used the Introduction to say that it was necessary to distinguish as clearly as possible between those moments in which the word "market" is being used as a concept for thinking through abstract theoretical relationships in economics and those moments in which it is being used as shorthand for a political ideology of governing that seeks a hands-off approach to managing the economy. Yet if there are, as I have subsequently argued in this chapter, at least three distinct market concepts existing side-by-side in economics, then this seems to mean that there must also be more than one way in which the market concept might be confused for the political ideology of "the market".

The specific structure of the descriptive market concept means that when this variant of the concept is in play the confusion is likely to be least pronounced. This, to recap, is the concept with eighteenth-century origins that treats the market as a physical marketplace and asks about the nature of the engagement therein between buyers and sellers. There is such a marked distinction in register between the use of this market concept and market ideology that the two should not be expected to be easily conflated with one another. However, it is also this use of the market concept that has almost entirely disappeared from economics except at its most heterodox margins. It receives almost no column inches in the textbooks that act as guides to teaching the subject field's underlying theoretical principles today. All of the action, so to speak, centres around the analytical and formalist market concepts, and it is here also that much of the confusion emerges about whether "the market" is being used conceptually or as an ideological claim about how best to reformulate the underlying essence of social relations. The following three chapters now proceed to flesh out these competing market concepts in turn.

CHAPTER 3

SYMMETRICAL MORAL RELATIONSHIPS
Adam Smith's impartial spectator construct

INTRODUCTION

> "He's pre-capitalist, a figure of the Enlightenment. What we would call capitalism he despised. People read snippets of Adam Smith, the few phrases they teach in school. Everybody reads the first paragraph of *The Wealth of Nations* where he talks about how wonderful the division of labor is. But not many people get to the point hundreds of pages later, where he says that division of labor will destroy human beings and turn people into creatures as stupid and ignorant as it is possible for a human being to be."
>
> Noam Chomsky, linguist and political activist

> "Even today – in blithe disregard of his actual philosophy – Smith is generally regarded as a *conservative* economist, whereas in fact, he was more avowedly hostile to the *motives* of businessmen than most New Deal economists."
>
> Robert Heilbroner, *The Worldly Philosophers*

There now exists something approaching a cottage industry of authors attempting to detail "what Adam Smith really meant". His text provides the most reliable insights into his thinking, but on its own it can only take us some of the way towards his innermost thoughts. To get the whole way would require explanations of the relationship between the content of his work, the specific context in which it was written and why his ideas were being propelled in a certain direction at a certain moment in time. Such an account could only have come from his own hand, but unfortunately these were not reflections that he left for his subsequent interpreters to mull over. Meanwhile, almost all generations since Smith's death in 1790 have put him to work trying to solve their problems as opposed to his. *The Wealth of Nations* is, after all, a famously open-ended book that permits multiple readings (Rothschild 2001). It acts almost as an invitation to read your own perspective into its pages, allowing later generations to persuade themselves that they have found there what they specifically set out to look for (Tribe 1999). Yet this means that they are positing a Smith of their own creation and not necessarily citing faithfully what he committed to the page in his own words. The original text of Smith's work therefore remains the best source material we have as an antidote to later self-serving readings.

It also reveals what from today's perspective looks like Smith's eclectic interests. He was writing at a time before social theory fragmented into separate disciplines in a process that often goes by the name of "professionalization" (Bernstein 2003). Accordingly, he made no attempt to restrict himself to trying to isolate the essentially economic components of behaviour, as generations of suitably professionalized academic economists have subsequently done. Indeed, it would be a stretch to say that there was such a thing as economics in Smith's day, and there certainly were no university positions in economics. Smith's first professorial appointment at the University of Glasgow in 1751 was to teach courses in logic, before he assumed the Chair in Moral Philosophy the next year (Kennedy 2008). However, he had already created a following for himself before securing an academic post. From 1748 he had delivered public lectures under the auspices of the Philosophical Society of Edinburgh, focusing to critical acclaim on matters as diverse as rhetoric and belles-lettres (I. S. Ross 2003). It is therefore perhaps only to be expected that the influences that Smith drew upon to write about the structure of economic life were extremely wide ranging.

The sheer breadth of Smith's work presents difficulties for the modern reader. If you open *The Wealth of Nations* for the first time being only familiar previously with the content of economics textbooks, you are likely to find it something of a surprise. You will almost certainly already have been told about Smith's reputation as the founder of modern economic theory, and you might also recall some sort of suggestion that everything that is to be studied as economics today follows in one sense or another from Smith. It is therefore somewhat disconcerting to dive into *The Wealth of Nations* for the first time and discover something the likes of which you have never seen before. Most people do not get very far on their initial encounter with its text before giving up on it, and its unfamiliar feel to the modern reader is the most important reason why it leaves anyone who thinks that they have been promised the foundational text for later economic analysis rather nonplussed. Smith's work has none of the diagrams that we find on almost every page of today's economics textbooks, and it also provides no evidence of the search for the essential characteristics of economic behaviour framed by the market concept. A good proportion of the pages are given over to theoretical development, but this is within the broader context of lengthy discussions of how the key policy-making dilemmas of the day can be thought of as moral puzzles.

If it will be in vain to search *The Wealth of Nations* for something approaching today's methods for economic enquiry, the same is also true of Smith's account of **market coordination**. This is a problem that has been somewhere in the background of economic theory for at least two and a half centuries now (Aydinonat 2008). It asks how might market institutions leave the impression of coordinated solutions when market-based decision-making is highly decentralized, being dispersed across many individuals who do not have the opportunity to come together beforehand to discuss their plans. Smith was by no means inattentive to this issue, because he was writing towards the beginning of the age of commercial society and could therefore see in front of him the transformations being wrought as more and more economic activity took place within market institutions (Justman 1993). Much of the historical analysis in *The Wealth of Nations* is actually a description of the way in which these changes had begun to exert a hold (Heilbroner 1986). The interesting thing in this regard, though, is that Smith's account of the **market coordination problem** is not to be found in *The Wealth of Nations* at all but in his earlier *Theory of Moral Sentiments*. As is maybe only to be expected of a Professor of Moral Philosophy, he established his discussion of the market concept not as a matter on which economic theory could adjudicate so much as a matter of moral theory (Watson 2005b). Perhaps this is another reason for the feeling of disorientation that many people feel on their initial attempt to engage with the text of *The Wealth of Nations*. Viewed from today's perspective at least, very little is as you would expect to find it; very little is even *where* you would expect to find it.

This chapter attempts to bring some clarity to the apparent riddle of how one of the most famous economists of all time could tackle the market coordination problem as something other than an intrinsically economic question. It proceeds in three stages. In section one I outline Smith's sympathy procedure, according to which acts of fellow-feeling might be used to foster increasingly symmetrical moral relationships for governing all aspects of social existence. He applied this way of thinking to the new marketplaces that were popping up all around in order to ask how the increasing prevalence of market institutions might serve as a factor of social cohesion. Section two deepens this mode of analysis to highlight just how different Smith's market concept was to what came next in the history of economic thought. Almost all economic theory after that time has pointed towards a market concept that reflects a pure economic essence, but Smith's market concept simply did not utilise the same basic ontology. This is not to say, however, that there are not glimpses of the route towards these subsequent developments within

The Wealth of Nations. Section three explores some of these complexities within the text. It shows that whilst Smith's own account of the market concept continued to be located in *The Theory of Moral Sentiments* right up until the final edition published in 1790, the year of his death, some parts of *The Wealth of Nations* did begin to flirt with the language of "demand and supply", which provides the foundations for the subsequent development of an analytical market concept. *The Wealth of Nations* is an amalgam of ideas that took shape over a prolonged period, and those elements that were conceived last are the most modern-looking when viewed from today's perspective.

THE IMPARTIAL SPECTATOR AND THE SYMPATHY PROCEDURE

"Adam Smith's image of competition in the marketplace was intended as an adjunct to his detailed description of human motivation in *The Theory of Moral Sentiments*, in which the pursuit of profit is tempered at every juncture by sympathy and benevolence, and by the posture of the 'impartial spectator' which is forced on us by our moral nature."

Ted Malloch, author of *Doing Virtuous Business*

"Smith's impartial spectator, considered as an inner man, is constructed by a process of internalisation of such outer people, using them as mirrors to reflect ourselves as we seek images of the proper action to take."

Alexander Broadie, "Sympathy and the Impartial Spectator"

Smith created a hypothetical entity called the **impartial spectator** to explain how a person might develop a pristine moral character (Raphael 2007). As recounted throughout his philosophical work, moral propriety is always a disposition that people need to nurture and continue to refine. They do not display a fully-formed capacity to do right by other people from day one. In Smith's (1982 [1759/1790]: III.6.11) words, "A man may learn to write grammatically by rule, with the most absolute infallibility; and so, perhaps, he may be taught to act justly". However, because the rules of grammar are "precise, accurate, and indispensable", whereas those of justice are "loose, vague, and indeterminate", the condition of moral propriety is one that most people take often faltering steps towards through a series of misfires. There will almost inevitably be occasions when they are sure that they have acted in an appropriate manner but the response from other people to those actions tells them something else entirely. Exhibiting the impartial spectator is a process that involves learning by doing, but also learning from your mistakes.

Smith believed that it was a strongly instinctive disposition in just about everybody to see other people's well-being as part of their own concern. The very first sentence of *The Theory of Moral Sentiments* says as much: "How selfish soever man may be supposed, there are evidently some principles in his nature, which interest him in the fortune of others, and render their happiness necessary to him, though he derives nothing from it except the pleasure of seeing it" (Smith 1982 [1759/1790]: I.i.1.1). But he did not assume that what was at heart hardwired into most people's character would necessarily ever be manifested in a perfect form without sustained self-tutelage. It is the expression of moral propriety every bit as much as its essence that we have to learn over time, and this process will require that we get things wrong repeatedly before developing a more fine-tuned sense of how to get things right. It is only once we get things right so often that most people's memories are of our actions being fault-free that we can say we have successfully developed our impartial spectator (Evensky 2005).

The impartial spectator is necessarily a part of the self, because it is the hypothetical entity that acts as a conscience figure and helps us to distinguish right from wrong and appropriate from inappropriate. Yet the very fact that Smith could talk about its existence on an abstract philosophical plane meant that he was operating with a fragmented conception of the self (Weinstein 2006). He wrote about the necessity for the urge to act partially to prefer oneself to be successfully countered by the opposing urge to act impartially if the individual was ever to be able to contribute to a stable and functioning society (Forman-Barzilai 2005). Both urges were natural and both entailed a learning process if what was in some way instinctive was ever to be refined so that a balance could be struck between the two elements of the self, hence leading the individual to avoid causing offence to other people.

The emphasis that Smith placed on nurturing the capacities of the impartial spectator showed that even though he thought that intuitions towards partiality and impartiality were both natural this did not mean that he also thought they exerted equal force. The morally untutored self, he argued, would always feel a more potent urge to act upon "the too partial views which self-love might otherwise suggest" (Smith 1982 [1759/1790]: III.4.12). Smith drew an evocative distinction between the "man without" and the "man within" in an attempt to explain how this tendency towards partiality might be corrected. On the one hand, the "man without" is the person who acts within society and whose behaviour, warts and all, is observed there by other people whose instincts for moral propriety are also imperfectly formed. The "man without" thus acts within the context of equally fallible peers who might give praise when none is due or withhold praise when it should rightfully be given. On the other hand, the "man within" embodies the unseen remonstrations that this same person has with themselves in private when

41

they are aware that their behaviour will meet with disapproval when viewed from the perspective of someone whose capacity for moral judgement is well honed (Smith 1982 [1759/1790]: III.2.32). It is worthy of comment that Smith (1982 [1759/1790]: I.iii.1.6) wrote rather regretfully of the "prodigious effort" that would be required for the "man without" to start meeting the standards of propriety insisted upon by a well-tutored "man within".

Smith's impartial spectator construct recognizes that we are at the same time both the responsible agents for our own decisions and a potential critic of how those decisions are likely to be received by other people. There is no surefire prescience involved here, and as a result we can never know exactly how our actions will be interpreted by everyone who is affected by them. However, we are not shooting in the dark every time we conduct ourselves in ways that have consequences beyond the immediacy of the self. Almost every action that we contemplate will have some sort of parallel in actions that we have undertaken sometime in the past. We should be able to scour our memory banks to call back to mind not only the cues we received from other people about whether this was appropriate behaviour, but also the degree to which these responses diverged from our expectations. According to Smith (1982 [1759/1790]: I.iii.1.14), it is the desire to close this gap between expected response and actual response that triggers the next stage of the process of moral self-tutelage. This is an iterative process that will not stop until there is perfect harmony between the "man without" and the "man within", and because this is such a difficult position to reach the process might actually never stop.

The impartial spectator is crucial to the account of Smith's *Theory of Moral Sentiments*, because it is only when it is a noticeable presence across the whole of society that the conditions of social stability are likely to ensue (Fitzgibbons 1995). A society in which everybody does as they please without a second's thought for how their actions will impact on other people is unlikely to be a cohesive social organism. This entails that everybody develops the capacity to think of themselves as being split down the middle, in Smith's (1982 [1759/1790]: III.1.6) words to separate "that I, the examiner and judge ... from that other I, the person whose conduct is examined into and judged of". The former, "the examiner and judge", counsels the self not to stray too far from the path of propriety, and it is up to the latter, "the person whose conduct is examined into and judged of", to heed those warnings and to prove that they can do right by other people. This necessarily involves subduing the emotions that promote partiality so that suitably moderated emotional behaviour might arise in its place. As the noted Smith scholar Andrew Skinner (1979: 51) has argued, the impartial spectator demands "a certain mediocrity of expression".

According to Smith, it is within the range of just about all of us to begin to develop the capacities of the impartial spectator (Ginzberg 2002). This is because it comes intuitively to everyone to live their lives observing what is going on around them without needing to put much thought to the process of doing so. At one level this might involve nothing more than the physical act of watching what other people do, but at another level it is about the more subtle practice of getting a feel from their words about what other people are really thinking. The opening premise on which the whole of Smith's moral theory resides is that we are all likely to conduct ourselves as spectators. The self-reflexivity that we need to exhibit if we are to learn how to become better versions of our former selves always has its origins in these spectatorial moments (Smith 1982 [1759/1790]: I.i.1.4). When this capacity is at its most advanced, it is possible to use it to pass judgement not only on actions once they have been taken, but also on intended action that has yet to occur. This latter ability requires us to play out in our mind the most likely scenario that will follow when the intended action is made real. It is therefore the source of the moderation that the impartial spectator implores when a pre-emptive understanding of what we would otherwise be about to do tells us that our conduct will not be well received (Smith 1982 [1759/1790]: I.i.5.8). We thus attain the heights of propriety in our moral conduct by turning inwards on ourselves the capacity for moral judgement that we first hone through observing the actions of other people.

The most basic spectatorial moments involve us being the third person in an unfolding relationship between the two main protagonists of an event. We have no direct involvement in that relationship and we are almost certainly not going to have an explicit stake in the way in which the event is played out. Even with this disinterested status, though, we are likely to find that we have taken note of both the action of one protagonist and the response to that action by the other protagonist. For instance, if we are standing in a marketplace contemplating how we are going to conduct our business for the day, we will discover that we are unintentionally privy to all sorts of other moments of exchange that have no direct bearing on our own reasons for being in that marketplace. We will overhear conversations that are not meant for our ears; we will also oversee interactions that are not meant for our eyes. Smith was adamant that it is natural to start passing judgement in situations such as this. If we are aware of both the action and the response it elicited, we will find it difficult not to ask ourselves whether the response was justified in the context of the initial action. How close have the protagonists come, in other words, to producing a situation in which prevailing standards of moral propriety would indicate that the observed response was perfectly in keeping with the observed action?

This whole way of thinking takes on even more profound implications when we go from being an actual observer of an event to learning how to pass moral judgement on events that we have only been able to observe vicariously. We live in an information-rich age where all sorts of new media help us to imagine what we would have felt had we been physically present as the event in question unfolded in real time. This enables us to experience an instinctive emotional response that would previously have been reserved for moments in which we had been on-the-spot spectators. Our engagement with historical studies can also be used to project ourselves vicariously back into situations that seem to demand we take a political stance.

Think back briefly to your instinctive reaction when confronted with the three historical examples with which the book began. Do you recall the outline of a moral judgement taking shape in your mind as the picture emerged of a clash of wills involving "the market"? All three examples are conventionally recounted as instances in which the veto power of "the market" was used to administer some sort of punishment beating. But what position did you alight on when deciding whether the retribution meted out by "the market" was appropriate, proportional and justified? In other words, what was your emotional response when projecting yourself vicariously back into the situations described in the three examples? Did Mitterrand deserve to be punished for trying to carry through the reform programme on which he had been elected? Did the five East Asian countries deserve to be punished for having a successful development model that in many ways stood outside mainstream western economic opinion? Did Bear Stearns deserve to be punished for having misread so calamitously price signals in the market for mortgage-backed securities?

Let me turn back now to the more generic case of the marketplace example. Here, the action of most interest is the emotional response to the observed relationship between a particular product and a particular price. We encounter these instances with such frequency that we may not always recognize them for what they are. If we have gone to make a purchase in a shop, for instance, then almost inevitably our eye will be drawn to other people's response on first seeing a price tag. If we are online we are likely to use the same instinct for observation to read the comments about product price left by other consumers. Both instances will cause thoughts about affordability and value for money to race through the brain. The situation that Smith described might well lead to very similar questions, but the process of exchange manifested itself differently. As reflected his day, he concentrated on instances in which buying and selling was a face-to-face activity and where the final transaction price was, at least to some degree, open to a process of negotiation. It seems a fairly obvious point to make that this is not the way in which most purchases are made today, but there are sufficient moments in which this is still the case to ensure that Smith's market concept remains relevant. In these moments, the advertised price does not necessarily translate into a hard-and-fast behavioural rule, so much as act as a guide to where the negotiation should begin over how much money will be necessary to transfer ownership of the product from the seller to the buyer. Most examples of negotiated prices today occur in those physical places that we still tend to call "markets" (or their cultural equivalent).

The question to bring to mind from Smith's perspective when observing this type of interaction is whether the person selling the product has responded in the morally appropriate manner in either accepting or rejecting the offer. The consumer with a fully-activated impartial spectator will only ever offer the exact intrinsic value of the product, which in Smith's (1981 [1776/1784]: I.vii.15) account covers the costs of production and provides a little more to allow the producer to take home some profits. Meanwhile, the producer with a fully-activated impartial spectator will instinctively only ever ask for this, the natural price, in the first place. A process of equilibration seems to be inferred, but it has nothing to do with the operation of market institutions, and certainly nothing to do with this thing called "the market". The key source of both consumer and producer knowing how to conduct an exchange in which neither loses out is both having learnt how to express themselves economically through the perspective of their impartial spectators. It is here we see how the market coordination problem as originally stated by Smith is not a problem that we should expect economic theory to provide an answer to, so much as one that is located in the realm of moral philosophy.

Moments at which nobody is asked to transact at anything other than the natural price are equivalent to those described in Smith's moral theory as moments of **mutual sympathy**. According to this theory, the reason we watch what other people do as part of our moral self-tutelage is because we have an inbuilt desire for the sensation of fellow-feeling (Fleischacker 2004). We have the capacity to swap places, if only ever vicariously, with the person we see respond to an event: what Smith (1982 [1759/1790]: VII. iii.1.4) called the "imaginary change of situations with the person principally concerned". We use the imagination to ask ourselves how we would have felt had the event just happened to us instead of them, and we create in our minds an imprint of the emotions we think that we would most likely have experienced had we been one of the main protagonists in the event. Smith (1982 [1759/1790]: I.i.4.7) called this the "secret consciousness" that results from "the change of situations". This can then be used as a benchmark against which to evaluate the response just witnessed, to judge whether its content, pitch and tone were about right for "the situation which excites it" (Smith 1982 [1759/1790]: I.i.1.10). It meets with our approbation when we arrive at a position where we can be sure from our own imaginative reconstruction of how we would have responded that the reaction we have just witnessed was appropriate. It is in this situation that we experience the sensation of emitting **sympathy** with the person most immediately affected by the event, where Smith's understanding of the sympathy procedure comes from the original Greek meaning of the word, "to feel with" (Montes 2003).

The condition of mutual sympathy requires us to go one step further. The marketplace example referred to previously often involves us either overhearing or overseeing someone else trying to strike the basis of a deal with which all concerned are satisfied. But what are we doing in that marketplace if not hoping to conduct some business of our own? Being privy to someone else's transaction is also a learning experience to tell us what we might have to expect when we also enter into negotiations over a price. If we swap places with a consumer who was clearly unimpressed with the price that they were quoted, do we think that the emotional display through which they conveyed their reluctance to part with that much money was justified? If we do, then we will feel sympathy with the consumer who has just walked away from the potential deal but not with the producer who has cited the price in question. We will only go ahead with the deal when we can assure ourselves that we will have those feelings of sympathy. A savvy producer will know this and, within Smith's framework at least, will consequently try to pitch their wares at a price that ensures sympathy all round.

MARKET COORDINATION FROM SMITH'S PERSPECTIVE

"Looking into someone's eyes changes the entire conversation."
"Sometimes, the eyes tell a story more than the tongue."

Anonymous

"Estimates vary as to how much tax revenue is lost by governments due to transfer mispricing. Global Financial Integrity in Washington estimates the amount at several hundred billion dollars annually."

Tax Justice Network website

For anyone whose only exposure to the market concept is through the economics textbooks, Smith's account is likely to come as a bolt out of the blue. It entails allowing the thought processes to flow in a completely new direction. The moment of mutual sympathy is every bit as much a conceptual abstraction as the point of equilibrium is in the analytical market concept that I am denoting as the Mk 2 phase. But the two do not have the same instinctive character attached to them. However hard we try, we are likely to struggle for an intuitive grasp of what a point of equilibrium might look like were we to experience one in practice (see Chapter 4), let alone the vector of equilibrium prices that generates the solution to general equilibrium in the formalist market concept (see Chapter 5). By contrast, a moment of mutual sympathy appears to be much less distant to what we are aware of experiencing in everyday life. I suspect that most of us would recognize a moment of mutual sympathy if we were to see it. It therefore gives the impression of being part of our everyday experience in a way that a point of equilibrium does not. Not all conceptual abstractions in economic theory, then, have the same degree of remoteness attached to them.

Bringing the market concept into people's everyday lives actually matches very nicely Smith's general account of scientific explanation. The role of explanation, he argued, was to construct bridges in the mind to allow the unknown to be viewed through the prism of something much more familiar (Smith 1982a: II.12). We only strive for new knowledge in the first place, he thought, because we are confronted with something that is outside our existing frame of reference (Fiori 2001). The trick to learning anything new about the world is to subject it to the test of something that we already know, to see it as a reflection of something that we believe we can already explain only too well. This is not necessarily about understanding the new thing in its essential form, so much as understanding enough about it to make it comprehensible as a neat replica of something else (Smith 1982a: II.11). This is evident in Smith's account of market coordination, through which he explained the relatively new phenomenon of market exchange as if it was governed by the same moral rules as all other forms of interpersonal interactions. If we know how to act in general in ways that do no harm to other people, he seems to have been saying, then this also serves as a permissible set of behavioural rules for engaging at the interpersonal level in the more specific setting of market institutions.

However, in its purest form at least, Smith's emphasis on spectatorial moments suggests the need for close physical proximity between the counterparties to the exchange. Presumably it is not too difficult to imagine how mutual sympathy might arise in such circumstances. It is well documented that the need to look someone in the eye when establishing the terms for an interaction is often enough in itself to lead to a moderation of the otherwise intended action. Of course, not everyone is affected in the same way by the promptings of conscience, as the process of activating the impartial spectator will be unevenly distributed across the population as a whole. Those people who are relatively unmoved by conscience might be expected to engage in commercial practices that will lead to immediate condemnation by the other counterparty for displaying overt partiality to the self. But where the process of self-reflexivity is more advanced, leading to greater engagement with the standards of moral propriety, it tends to be more difficult to summon up the nerve to deliberately hoodwink someone, especially if you are interested in securing their repeat custom. Close physical proximity is therefore likely to make a difference to the informal rules of conduct that help to regulate marketplace behaviour. What happens, though, when the marketplace in question bears none of those physical characteristics, when observation of a direct nature is simply not possible? What effect does this have on a spectatorial theory of market coordination?

It certainly means that the most we can expect is for observation via proxy, rather than direct observation where the person principally concerned can physically see all of the other people who are counterparties to the exchange. Indeed, global value chains are now so stretched across space that the consumer is almost certainly going to have no idea of the identity of the producer for anything other than the most locally made products. However, Smith becomes a far from straightforward interlocutor at this point. The stretching of global value chains across space inevitably takes away some of the potency of the spectatorial moment, which is necessarily a bad thing according to his moral theory. At the same time, though, the very first page of *The Wealth of Nations* argues that: "The greatest improvement in the productive powers of labour, and the greater part of the skill, dexterity, and judgment with which it is any where directed, or applied, seem to have been the effects of the division of labour" (Smith 1981 [1776/1784]: I.i.1). As this improvement is linked throughout his work to the ability to lift people out of poverty, successive enhancements of the division of labour are always a good thing according to Smith's economic theory. Later in Book I of *The Wealth of Nations*, he stated that "the division of labour ... must always be limited ... by the extent of the market" (Smith 1981 [1776/1784]: I.iii.1). It is these geographical constraints that the stretching of global value chains across space is designed to circumvent, which appears to place this process in the curious position of deserving a thumbs up from the perspective of Smith's economic theory but a thumbs down from the perspective of his moral theory.

Many firms, especially the largest, have recently found that it is beneficial to their financial bottom line to view the production process as a series of discrete stages, each of which might be located in a different country if that is what it takes to keep its overall production costs down (Gereffi 2014). A good proportion of world trade is actually trade conducted by two parts of the same company in pursuit of bringing a single product to the marketplace (Gupta 2017). All sorts of tax loopholes can be exploited in this way by "overpricing" those elements of the production process that take place in low-tax environments and "underpricing" those elements that take place in high-tax environments (Corrick 2016). So much, then, for Smith's dream of a world of such advanced impartial spectators that the natural price would reign supreme. His own principle of the division of labour as it is applied today helps to force prices away from their natural level whilst simultaneously immobilizing the spectatorial capacities that might act as a counter-tendency. Modern-day firms can never lose out from this **transfer pricing** strategy of overpricing in some circumstances and underpricing in others, because they are only ever trading with themselves. The most obvious loser is the national tax authority, which is still required to fund the **public goods** that allow businesses to make money but is deprived of significant business contributions to the tax system (Sikka & Willmott 2010; Brooks 2013).

Another loser is likely to be the person who demands of themselves that they activate their impartial spectator in as many commercial environments as possible. By the time that a single product has gone through all of these elements of the production process, it would be unreasonable to expect that the consumer of the final product will be able to name the other people involved in the production process at a distinctly personal level. That consumer will be aware of trading with the firm but not of being able to look the producer in the eye at the moment of making the exchange, as would have been the case in the eighteenth-century marketplaces of which Smith wrote directly. As a consequence, the spectatorial moment is broken in an explicitly interpersonal sense and an increasing amount of everyday economic life is conducted in strictly anonymized form, away from the reach of the impartial spectator.

We can see the significance of the rise of anonymized market relations in how much effort is made in the name of ethical consumption to strategically de-anonymize the moment of exchange. The value of products bought and sold under the Fairtrade mark has grown enormously since fair trade accreditation was all brought under the same international standard only twenty years ago (Raynolds, Murray & Wilkinson 2007). The most recent figures available are for 2015, when the monetary value of Fairtrade purchases rose by one-seventh to pass the symbolically important €1 billion barrier for the first time (Fairtrade International 2017). Such a surge in sales has developed alongside, and reflects the success of, a more general political narrative of fair trade that has been constructed by a variety of global justice advocates. This narrative is perhaps not as prominent now as it once was, because the new trend for Fairtrade advertising is for plain packaging with some celebrity endorsements thrown into the mix. For some time, though, most Fairtrade products had pictures of the type of person who would stand to benefit from the purchase of those products emblazoned across their packaging. This would be accompanied by the farmer introducing you to their family, to the aspirations they had for their children and to the social infrastructure that the commercial success of their products was helping to provide for the community as a whole (Watson 2007). The spectatorial moment was not wholly restored in instances such as these, because at most it was possible for the consumer to experience fellow-feeling with the image of the *type* of person on the other side of the exchange rather than the *actual* person who had, say, planted and picked the coffee beans in the case of Fairtrade coffee. But it is still a spectatorial moment of sorts, at least to the extent to which it allows the consumer to demonstrate to themselves that their impartial spectator has been activated. Even now that this self-consciously de-anonymized packaging is no longer such a visible feature of Fairtrade products, the surrounding political narrative of fair trade remains familiar.

There is also now plenty of evidence of how unsettling it can be for any firm to be on the receiving end of coordinated disruptive consumer behaviour (Richter 2001). A consumer boycott operates as an often extremely effective way of exerting pressure for more obviously conscionable action on the part of firms (Clouder & Harrison 2005). No company wants to hear that its ethical credentials are being questioned to such a degree that what it once took to be its loyal customer base is now in open revolt. However, very few firms with a genuinely global reach have ever managed to escape all such scrutiny. This might be due to historical misdemeanours, such as profiteering from wars or acting as a conduit for empire, or it might be triggered by a sense that its practices in the present are being driven by an openly exploitative agenda. One such agenda today revolves around the tax issue. Firms will try to present themselves to government enquiries as good corporate citizens who have all the necessary paperwork to show that they are paying all the tax for which they are liable in each national jurisdiction, whereas tax justice advocates will show how this has translated into triggering loopholes whereby their overall tax payments are miniscule compared with what they should be on a pro rata calculation based on sales numbers (Shaxson 2011). The list is long indeed of the globally-recognisable brands that have experienced consumer-led campaigns aimed at regularizing tax payments across firms of all sizes (Alexander 2015).

Still, though, it is necessary to say a few words about the way in which the pseudo-spectatorial moments described here differ morally from those that Smith thought might lead to socially cohesive market relations. He believed that there would be a genuine desire on the part of both counterparties to act reputably and, more importantly, to become known as the sort of person who could be trusted to act reputably (Force 2003). Commercial advantage, after all, was dependent on tempting people back into repeat transactions in the days when to act within a marketplace meant acting in a direct face-to-face manner. Commercial advantage today, by contrast, often seems to be about firms doing the bare minimum to prove that they have stayed on the right side of the borderline between what is and what is not legal and then hoping that this is enough not to trigger more all-encompassing consumer disruption. Firms will give voice to good intentions today to try to get by without suffering further damage to their reputation and correspondingly further desertion from their consumer base.

The spectatorial moments that contribute to conduct in modern-day marketplaces therefore look to be decidedly one-sided. Where they take anything approaching the character described by Smith, it seems to be that they are being pushed almost wholly by consumers. It is consumers who typically define what it might take for them to be able to assure themselves that they are acting ethically in the myriad virtual marketplaces in which they are likely to be participants nowadays. It is also consumers, then, who bring into being generalized perceptions of the conditions that would have to be in place for ethical exchange to become a feature of everyday economic life. Firms, by contrast, tend to be purely reactive agents in this process. They are not usually making the running and, whenever evidence tends to be forthcoming that they have acted as if an impartial spectator was in play, this often feels as though it was a step entered into only begrudgingly. The rating of online retailers is a good case in point. Producers might well point after-the-fact to how these ratings justify their claims to be a reputable counterparty. However, they were set up in the first place as a means of allowing consumers to alert one another to the dangers of trading with particular producers. In eighteenth-century marketplaces where close physical proximity was the order of the day, they might well have been able to send this sort of signal through emotive responses that they would have known would be seen and heard. Now, though, ratings that can be read by anyone with access to the internet serve the same purpose. It should be noted, however, that the reverse does not apply. There is no real equivalent of mass participation online sites through which retailers rate their customers.

SMITH AND THE LANGUAGE OF "DEMAND AND SUPPLY"

"[M]any people ... regard the phrase 'supply and demand' as synonymous with economics ... But surprisingly few people actually understand what the phrase means. In a debate about health care, poverty, recent events in the stock market, or the high price of housing, you might hear someone say, 'Well, it's just a matter of supply and demand,' as a way of dismissing the issue entirely. Others use the phrase with an exaggerated reverence, as if supply and demand were an inviolable physical law, like gravity, about which nothing can be done."

Robert Hall and Marc Lieberman,
Economics: Principles and Applications

"Corporations cannot act philanthropically in America. It is against the law. They cannot act altruistically. They have to have, always, the profit motive in mind."

Robert Kennedy Jr, radio host, author and activist

Modern-day producers who are confronted by consumers insisting that they conduct themselves in line with more exacting ethical standards than are currently visible in their behaviour tend to answer the charge in a different register to the one in which it is put to them. They typically find themselves being engaged at the level of moral discourse and being asked to imagine their future actions from within the boundaries set by this discourse. Instead of responding like-for-like, however, it is almost always the case that they will position themselves in some sense beyond the boundaries within which the challenge was laid down. Perhaps this is because they fear that they will be on a hiding to nothing if they try to defend their existing ethical standards using the same sort of moral language that was used in the first place to denounce them. Rather, it is much more likely that they will respond in a technical manner, citing what they believe to be the ethically-neutral language of "demand and supply" to do so. It is as if they think that they can turn the argument back in their favour with a dispassionate account of prevailing economic conditions. Abiding by the logic of "the market", after all, makes attention to these conditions the firm's first obligation to its shareholders.

Political debates about the permissible degree of encroachment of "the market" within society thus often take place across incommensurable registers. There are those who insist that the logic of "the market" should not be used as a catchall excuse to allow private sector operators to do exactly as they please regardless of the social, cultural and environmental consequences of their economic actions. Their register is undoubtedly ethical in its underlying orientation, disregarding the opposing claims that efficiency shortfalls will inevitably ensue if ethical obligations are imposed on producers to a degree that is beyond that which "the market" can be expected to bear. The alternative register is straightforwardly economic, elevating efficiency considerations to the point at which they out-trump everything else. More exacting ethical standards might very well remain nice to contemplate, but they are depicted from this latter perspective as a luxury that the economy can ill afford. The much more integrated national economies of today compared to those of Smith's time have allowed for the process of **regulatory arbitrage** to occur, whereby one country can gain a possibly enormous commercial advantage for its producers if it is willing to relax a degree of regulatory oversight that other countries seek to keep in place. Regulations tend to increase costs of production, which means that a producer facing fewer regulations than their competitors will likely be provided with a cost advantage akin to a subsidy.

Thinking in terms of these two registers, the ethical and the economic, it might be tempting to believe from the earlier sections of this chapter that Smith's work, with its close association to the descriptive market concept, belongs only to the former. It might therefore also be necessary to wait for the development of the analytical market concept and its associated demand-and-supply diagram before the move is made to the alternative economic register. However, we should not pre-empt this conclusion without further investigation. The two market concepts remain resolutely distinct, but there is a good case for saying that outlines of the second are just about visible in *The Wealth of Nations*, even though the majority of the book reflects the first. Smith, it could be argued, came close to having one foot in each of the two camps.

We know from the discovery and subsequent publication of two sets of student notes taken at his University of Glasgow lectures in 1762–3 and 1766 respectively that Smith used the words "demand" and "supply" in very close proximity to one another when attempting to explain basic economic laws. In their very first outing together he explained the case of how basic inequality of resources determines who gets to consume available goods, even if "there be two persons equally in fancy with any thing and equally earnest to have it". Concluding that "[t]he richest ... will always get it as he is best able to bid high(e)st", Smith (1982b: A.vi.71-2) argued that: "The price [and in this context he meant the market price] is in this manner regulated by the demand and the quantity there is to supply this demand; and whenever the quantity is not sufficient the price will be regulated by the fortunes of those who are the purchasers". Immediately, then, we should be attentive to the fact that his attempts to capture the basic essence of how the economy worked involved something very different to the description of the interpersonal relationships that helped to solve the market coordination problem. These might very well appear to be one and the same thing, but a detailed reading of Smith's texts suggests that he appealed to two different conceptual languages in his attempts to explain ostensibly the same process. It has long been a puzzle for specialist Smith scholars that the conceptual language of *The Theory of Moral Sentiments* is not imported directly to establish the conceptual puzzles that he sought to resolve in *The Wealth of Nations* (Keppler 2010). The essence of that language is visible on many occasions, if only implicitly, and it is here that Smith continued to focus on the collectively-bargained rules to which marketplaces would have to operate if they were not to impede social cohesion. When he discussed underlying economic laws in *The Wealth of Nations*, however, there is a noticeable change of register. It is, admittedly, more subtle than the change of register that results when corporate spokespeople today try to answer the request that they reinvent themselves as improved versions of their former moral selves with observations about the imperatives of "demand and supply". But it is a change of register nonetheless.

Once more, though, it is necessary not to rush to judgement. Smith's Glasgow lectures are well known to have provided the basis for much of the analysis that was subsequently published in *The Wealth of Nations* (Campbell & Skinner 1976; Meek, Raphael & Stein 1978). However, in the 1760s this was not yet the modern noun couplet "demand and supply". His use of "demand" as a noun is little different in essence to how we tend to see that word being used in economics today. It was still by no means exactly the same, because it lacked the precision that economists have brought to it today, but still it definitely looks to be of the same basic lineage. By contrast, at this time he used "supply" not as a noun but as a verb. Many of these examples survived pretty much intact to appear in Smith's famous Chapter VII of Book I of *The Wealth of Nations*. For instance, he wrote there that: "When the quantity of any commodity which is brought to market [there is that phrase "brought to market" again, see Chapter 2] falls short of the effectual demand, all those who are willing to pay the whole value of the rent, wages, and profit, which must be paid in order to bring it thither, cannot be supplied with the quantity which they want" (Smith 1981 [1776/1784]: I.vii.9). This is a conceptual language that invokes both demand and supply, then, but careful consideration shows that it is not today's language of "demand and supply".

As William Thweatt (1983) has shown, Sir James Steuart (1966 [1767]) was the first person to go at least some of the way towards closing the gap with the language that appears in contemporary economics teaching texts. He used the nouns "demand" and "supply" together seventeen times in his 1767 *Inquiry into the Principles of Political Economy*. Whether he was genuinely conscious of having done so in a manner that pre-empts modern usage, however, is another matter entirely. He had, after all, used the expression "quantity and demand" much more often in the same book, this phrase having been pioneered by John Law at the turn of the eighteenth century (see Murphy 1997). Besides, by the later nineteenth century when innovations in the use of the demand-and-supply diagram had been laid down, Steuart's work was remembered positively only amongst the various national historical schools of economics, and they were stridently opposed to the new marginalist way of thinking (Grimmer-Solem 2003). There is no clear line of connection here, then, to link the modern use of the demand-and-supply diagram to the first appearance together in an economic theory text of the words "demand and supply". Smith does appear to have used the noun couplet "demand and supply" more self-consciously than Steuart in chapters of *The Wealth of Nations* that historians of economic thought suspect were first drafted sometime after the Glasgow Lectures and possibly very close to the book's eventual 1776 publication date. Steuart therefore probably deserves to be given priority in first putting the phrase together, but it might belong to Smith when thinking about how it was first used self-consciously. Even then, though, the appearance side by side within *The Wealth of Nations* of two very different uses of the pair of words "demand" and "supply" does not help to clarify matters.

Peter Groenewegen (1973) has suggested that it was David Ricardo in his 1817 *Principles of Political Economy* who was the first person to use the noun couplet in a way that is recognisably similar to today's usage. But still this cannot be the end of the qualifications. Ricardo (2004 [1817/1821]: 119) certainly did use "demand and supply" in his explanation of short-run market prices: "It should be recollected that prices always vary in the market, and in the first instance, through the comparative state of demand and supply". This was the price level that Smith (1981 [1776/1784]: I.vii.15) believed was susceptible to what he called the "accidents" through which harm could be inflicted onto one of the parties to the exchange. The strictly economic element of his definition of harm referred to a situation in which the prevailing price had been deliberately driven away from long-run natural exchange values. Like Smith before him, Ricardo (2004 [1817/1821]: 88–93) worked with a conceptual distinction between market and natural prices, and he had a cost-of-production theory of the natural price. "[T]he prices of commodities," he argued, "which are subject to competition, and whose quantity may be increased in any moderate degree, will ultimately depend, not on the state of demand and supply, but on the increased or diminished cost of their production" (Ricardo 2004 [1817/1821]: 385). The noun couplet "demand and supply" was therefore definitely present in economic theory prior to the development of the demand-and-supply diagram – as, of course, would have to be the case as a matter of basic chronology – but it could hardly be said at that time to have been established in its modern form.

This leads to a series of complications when trying to think about the history of the market concept. It is often the case that a text like *The Wealth of Nations*, which has long been argued to sit at the intersection of two different traditions in economic theory, will tend to reveal glimpses of what was subsequently to become fleshed out by later writers as the newer tradition eventually comes to dominate. As the famed Smith scholar Jacob Viner (1989 [1928]: 126) observed in an essay written in the 1920s to commemorate the one hundred and fiftieth anniversary of the first edition of *The Wealth of Nations*, "traces of every conceivable sort of doctrine are to be found in that most catholic book". "[A]n economist must have peculiar theories indeed", he continued, "who cannot quote from [it] to support his special purposes". Often, though, this will entail the self-interestedly strategic reading back into Smith's text of pre-emptions of the commentator's own position. Smith is, after all, a leading authority figure in the history of economic theory, and to appropriate for reasons of enhancing your own credibility his reputation as the originator of the modern discipline is a well-rehearsed tactic. However, it is also not a particularly well-regarded tactic, because it usually entails taking snippets from the text and treating these as its overall voice, whilst at the same time conveniently ignoring everything else that appears to talk from a different analytical perspective.

It is much better to be thinking in terms of the balance of the work as a whole. Viewed in this way, the only conclusion to draw is that all of Smith's reflections on the market coordination problem inhabit the frame of the descriptive market concept, even if there are in addition some intriguing previews of a different conceptual language at those points in *The Wealth of Nations* where he began to discuss abstract economic laws. A case could possibly still be made that Smith consequently managed to speak in incommensurable ethical and economic registers within the text of *The Wealth of Nations*. Yet it also has to be recognized that these distinct registers are by no means equally applied in the frequency with which they appear there. It is the exception rather than the rule when Smith parts company with the market concept in its distinctively descriptive form to talk about the generic properties of pricing dynamics.

CONCLUSION

> "*The Theory of Moral Sentiments* is a global manifesto of profound significance to the interdependent world in which we live."
>
> Amartya Sen, "The Economist Manifesto"

> "We're supposed to worship Adam Smith but you're not supposed to read him. That's too dangerous. He's a dangerous radical."
>
> Noam Chomsky, linguist and political activist

The market concept in its descriptive phase must be treated as a distinct entity worthy of investigation in its own right. It is a concept that emphasizes the interpersonal characteristics of face-to-face exchanges within physical marketplaces. The question that animates it is one of moral philosophy rather than of economics as that subject field is practiced today: what degree of restraint must be accepted in the interests of creating perfectly symmetrical market relations in which both counterparties would happily accept either side of the exchange. This tradition is by no means exclusively synonymous with the work of Adam Smith, because the principle of avoiding the imposition of harm had a large number of proponents in the eighteenth century.

However, Smith's work remains an interesting route into the relevant arguments, in particular because of its apparent one-foot-in-two-camps phenomenon when read as a whole. This forces us to confront a big question. Is it possible to speak in an ethical and an economic register simultaneously, or will you always be forced to choose one over the other? The later history of the market concept as we move to its analytical phase seems to suggest that a subsequent generation of economists threw their lot in with a decidedly economic register. Smith, by contrast, appears to have opted for a much more eclectic approach. And there is nothing to make us think that this was not a conscious choice. He updated *The Wealth of Nations* on several occasions following its first publication, and at no stage in these later editions did he alter the fundamental balance between his ethical and economic registers. On the one hand, the ethical register was maintained whenever he wished to discuss the interpersonal processes through which functioning long-term market relations were forged. On the other hand, the economic register was used at those moments when he seems to have flirted most openly with the language of fundamental economic laws.

The Market Concept Mk 1 stands alone, then, as the only overwhelmingly descriptive version to have reached a position of prominence in the history of economic thought. It is therefore the variant that is most divorced from the contemporary political rhetoric of "the market" and its invocation of a thingified logic that commands obedience from all who fall under its sway. In Smith's hands at least it is wildly at odds with this rhetoric by suggesting that it is up to the market participants to take responsibility for themselves for the context in which they will have to learn how to operate. They will set the terms for their own behaviour by collectively negotiating with other market participants the parameters of admissible conduct to which they can all agree. There is no external force called "the market" that bears down upon them and takes this responsibility on itself by enforcing conformity of thought and conformity of action. Descriptive accounts of the market concept depict market relations as a much more obviously do-it-yourself feature of everyday economic life. They are to be made by the people who stand to either gain or lose from them and they are made against the backdrop of each participant's conscience telling them whether whatever gains they come to make are morally legitimate. There is no blithely following some abstract logic and hiding behind the idea that it is informing you about what to do and how to present yourself. The political language of "the market" breaks down irrevocably in the context of treating market relations in this way. Thingification is simply not possible when starting from this point.

However, it has also been shown that the changing structures of production and consumption within the world economy mean that it would be very difficult to live life today entirely in line with Smith's market abstraction.

There are still enough instances of face-to-face negotiations over fair prices to think that his descriptive market concept is more than merely a historical relic, but it would be extremely difficult to limit yourself to acting *only* within exchange relations of this type. On far more occasions you are likely to face the anonymized experience of interacting with an impersonal price structure. The stretching of production relations across space compounds the lack of knowledge of whose lives you are involving yourself in when going through the daily routine of making purchases. One would therefore struggle to use Smith's descriptive market concept as a template for everyday economic life today. But at the same time it still offers itself as an aspirational device for anyone who wants to resist the fatalistic assumption that navigating one's way through that life is simply about accommodating oneself in submissive manner to "the market".

There are reasons to continue to appeal to Smith's descriptive market concept, then, precisely because it represents something other than a purely economic register. The economy is an aspect of everyday life that will continue to be struggled over politically for as long as people still want to ask where they would most like the limits of "the market" to be fixed. That struggle in turn requires the ability to talk about market relations in a way that does not simply invoke a determining economic essence. It might not always be fashionable today to demand that conscience be involved when contemplating market-based decisions, let alone to make the argument directly through the lens of Smith's hypothetical impartial spectator. Yet there remain lots of people who are willing to object rather vociferously to the idea that the logic of "the market" exonerates all unconscionable behaviour. Firms will indeed want to make profits, producers will want to reduce their operating costs if at all possible, shareholders will want to see their investments pay off, consumers will always want to get the best deal they can, and so the list of desires that can be recounted in a purely economic register goes on. That register suggests that there is a fundamentally economic essence that underpins all human conduct in the commercial realm, but this looks more like excuse-making than it does a genuine description of what goes through people's minds when they are thinking about how to act economically. Presumably the possibility of how best to avoid harming other people enters into their consciousness to at least some degree.

This is where the descriptive market concept comes back into its own by restoring to prominence the ethical register. Following Smith at least, it forces us to ask what market relations would look like were they to be modelled on a situation to which the impartial spectator would be bound to give its consent. That is, what would result from striving for a situation in which each of the counterparties is sufficiently convinced of the moral symmetry of the exchange as to be willing to take either position in relation to it? This can then act as a benchmark for adjudicating on the propriety of the actual market relations in which we are involved today. Thinking about them descriptively asks us to consider how far away from moral symmetry they are. It also forces us to consider how far away from moral symmetry underlying conditions need to be before we would be of a mind to mobilize politically against them in the hope of a rather less one-sided experience of everyday economic life.

CHAPTER 4

DEMAND AND SUPPLY IN PARTIAL EQUILIBRIUM
The Marshallian cross diagram

INTRODUCTION

"I had a growing feeling in the later years of my work at the subject that a good mathematical theorem dealing with economic hypotheses was very well unlikely to be good economics."

Alfred Marshall, letter to Arthur Bowley, 1906

"Though a skilled mathematician, he [Marshall] used mathematics sparingly. He saw that excessive reliance on this instrument might lead us astray in pursuit of intellectual toys, imaginary problems not conforming to the conditions of real life."

Arthur Cecil Pigou, Marshall's successor as Professor of Political
Economy at Cambridge, Memorials of Alfred Marshall

Alfred Marshall spent most of his academic career at the University of Cambridge, eventually retiring as Professor of Political Economy there in 1908 after more than forty years' academic service within the UK. He was an important theorist in his own right, but he is perhaps best remembered today as a brilliant synthesizer of existing ideas, bringing flashes of insight from various parts of the literature into a single theoretical system (Hodgson 2001). More than anybody else, he was responsible for fleshing out the contributions that various marginalist techniques could be expected to make to economic theory as if they had all come from the same hand (Maloney 1991). The ideas on which he drew were therefore by no means all his own, although he did put his distinctive gloss on them in his renowned book, *The Principles of Economics*. It went through eight editions, eventually totalling 870 pages, and it was quickly seized upon as the authoritative text for learning about the market concept in what I have called its analytical form. For a number of decades it was as if economics in its orthodox Anglophone guise was specifically Marshallian. George Stigler published his *Theory of Price* in 1946 and Paul Samuelson his *Economics* in 1948 in an attempt to dislodge Marshall's *Principles of Economics* as the dominant teaching text. Their aim was that they might showcase the work of a newer generation of neoclassical economists.

So great were Marshall's skills as a synthesizer that theoretical discoveries were often attributed to him retrospectively, even when they had appeared earlier in their original form in someone else's writings. Nowhere is this better illustrated than in the case of the standard demand-and-supply diagram that still dominates introductory teaching texts in economics today. When it is given a definite name it always tends to be called the Marshallian cross diagram. This refers to its shape when it is drawn onto the two-dimensional space within which it is represented visually (see Chapter 2), the demand and supply curves being depicted as straight lines and allowed to intersect in the middle so that they might create a point of equilibrium (Marshall 1975 [1870]: 156–7). Marshall (2013 [1890/1920]: 290, 442) did not use this terminology himself, preferring to say that the demand and supply curves can be thought of as the two blades of a pair of scissors that are joined at the point of equilibrium. The Marshallian cross diagram is therefore sometimes called the Marshallian scissors diagram instead, where the common denominator is clearly the allusion to its specifically Marshallian nature. Yet this naming process on its own only means that he was the person who proved themselves most adept at drawing the analogy that turned the classic demand-and-supply diagram into an aspect of theoretical common sense. This, of course, is an entirely separate process from first having elaborated the underlying theoretical model.

Marshall certainly had predecessors, and one of the interesting aspects of his presentation of the demand-and-supply diagram is actually how it departed from that of many of the theorists who beat him to committing this way of thinking to paper. When the route from the predecessors' work to Marshall's is recovered today, it is invariably as part of attempts to specify the history of an avowedly mathematical approach to economic theory (Weintraub 2002). Yet Marshall's presentation of the demand-and-supply diagram does not appear to be overtly mathematical. He was by any standard a gifted mathematician, ending up as second wrangler during his undergraduate days at Cambridge (Cook 2009). The tradition at that time was for students taking the mathematical tripos to be placed in rank order on the basis of their performance in the final examinations and to have the name "wrangler" attached to their rank, from the senior wrangler down. Marshall's position as second wrangler in 1865 therefore means that only one of his student cohort bettered his performance, which bears favourable comparison, for instance, with John Maynard Keynes's position as twelfth wrangler within his student cohort forty years later. Despite this, and despite his predecessors' use of their own variants of the demand-and-supply diagram to try to trigger a step change in the mathematization of economic principles, Marshall's (2013 [1890]: xxiii) methodological choice was instead to keep the mathematics very much in the background.

The visual similarities between the various early articulations of the demand-and-supply diagram should not lead to this important difference being overlooked (Humphrey 1992). Marshall's predecessors used it precisely *because* it facilitated the enhanced treatment of economics as a mathematical science. It therefore tends to appear in their work only after the relationships to which they refer have first been described using algebraic equations. Marshall, by contrast, appears to have used the demand-and-supply diagram *in spite of* the ease with which it can be transposed into mathematical form. It is significant that he did not present it side by side with the accompanying mathematical explanation of what can be seen, let alone allowing the mathematics to take precedence in the running order of the text. Marshall's (2013 [1890/1920]: 297) treatment of the demand-and-supply diagram is entirely consistent with his general methodological position that the mathematics should be relegated to appendices and that "the main outlines [of economic theory] can [and, indeed, should] be presented in ordinary language". However, it was not consistent with either what went before or what came later.

This has led to an element of ambiguity that has by no means been eliminated in the century since Marshall's death. It is an ambiguity that goes right to the heart of what we are able to take from the market concept in its analytical form. The Marshallian cross diagram has become such a staple expression of the market concept understood analytically that, for so many generations of economics students learning their art through the textbooks, this is the only account of market principles that really matters. But what does it represent? The textbook answer is that it captures the essence of all economic problems in providing insights into the relationship between demand and supply (Jehle & Reny 2001). However, this rather begs the bigger question of whether "demand" and "supply" refer in this instance to categories that belong unequivocally to the real world or merely to theorists' self-made abstract worlds. That is, "demand" and "supply" might be said to relate to observable conditions in operation when actual stocks of a particular good are being bought and sold, or they might alternatively be said to relate to generic buying and selling principles through which efficiency gains might materialize. Two questions therefore become relevant in trying to decipher which is which in any given circumstances. Is the Marshallian cross diagram a representation of a fundamental economic essence that just so happens to also lend itself to mathematical formulation? Or is it a representation of a basic mathematical logic that it has become conventional to attach economic meaning to? Marshall's predecessors presented their original demand-and-supply diagrams as if the answer was "no" to the former question and "yes" to the latter. Marshall, by contrast, acted as if the reverse was true. Meanwhile, today's economics textbooks do little to resolve this tension. There are only infrequent attempts to show how the relationships captured by the Marshallian cross diagram can be translated into mathematical form, whilst still insisting that beginning economics students will prepare themselves better for what lies ahead the quicker they accept that their subject field operates intrinsically to a mathematical logic.

In an attempt to investigate these issues further, this chapter now proceeds in three stages. In the first section I show that the Marshallian cross diagram had a history before the publication of the first edition of Marshall's *Principles of Economics* in 1890. This makes him no less important to the way in which it subsequently entered the common sense of economics, but Marshall's grand synthesis is still best understood through the perspective of the rather staccato history of the demand-and-supply diagram that preceded it. Sections two and three reveal what more can be learned about the market concept in its analytical form by placing Marshall's treatment back into conversation with that of his predecessors. Section two focuses on the assumptions about economic agency that have to be made if the dynamics of the demand-and-supply diagram are to be underpinned by consistent behavioural axioms. It is shown that the primary feature of these hypothetical economic agents is how unrealistic we must assume their behaviour to be, as they are perfect embodiments of an abstract economic rationality. Section three begins to unpack some of the main criticisms, both from within economics and beyond, of economists' willingness to hang so much on the assumption of perfectly rational agents. Wherever possible the discussion will be returned to the major theme of the book, the relationship between the market concept and market ideology.

MARSHALL AND HIS PREDECESSORS

"Alfred Marshall, Cambridge's great economist at the turn of the [twentieth] century, helped forge these tools of supply and demand."

Paul Samuelson, *Economics*

"Marshall popularized ... the modern diagrammatic approach to economics."

Robert Sexton, *Exploring Microeconomics*

The classic demand-and-supply diagram takes such little explanation because it seems to speak to a series of economic processes that require no formal economic training for them to be rendered intelligible. Even the language of demand and supply is such a ubiquitous element of everyday economic discourse that it generally does not take people much to understand their decisions in relation to it. They do not need to have ever drawn on a new supply curve to the right of the original one to have an intuitive feeling that if new, low-cost production is made possible for consumer goods through the outsourcing of production within the global economy, then they are likely to have enhanced opportunities of buying that good at a lower price. This corresponds to the move along the original demand curve from A to B occasioned by the new position of the supply curve in the first of the two diagrams in Figure 4.1, such that the quantity demanded increases from Q_0 to Q_1 whilst the market price falls from P_0 to P_1. By the same token, they do not need to have plotted a leftward shift in the demand curve onto the standard two-dimensional representational space to be aware that if they work in an industry that is subject to this sort of outsourcing then jobs like theirs are likely to become less plentiful and also pay rather less. This corresponds to the move along the original supply curve from A to B occasioned by the new position of the demand curve in the second of the two diagrams in Figure 4.1, such that the number of jobs fall from Q_0 to Q_1 whilst the market wage rate also falls from P_0 to P_1. The language of demand and supply is too well known for these effects to have to be spelt out explicitly. This level of familiarity is also an important component of the jump between the market concept and treating "the market" as if it had a mind of its own to determine the results that it sought to impose. If "the market" is seen as having demand and supply curves that adjust automatically to changes in external economic conditions,

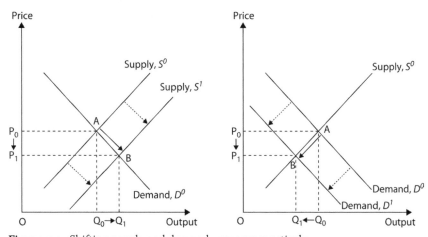

Figure 4.1: Shifting supply and demand curves respectively

then its judgement is not to be second-guessed and its will is simply to be accommodated.

It is important, however, not to make the mistake of thinking that for as long as people have wanted to write about the economy they have been able to rely on the language of demand and supply to do so. This is not a language that is somehow inherent in nature and simply needed the introduction of market institutions for its outline to spontaneously come into view. Like all other human languages it is an invented tradition designed to reflect a reality whose features are defined by social convention. As the final section of the previous chapter showed, historians of economic thought have spilt much ink trying to provide a comprehensive picture of how the language of demand and supply entered economics. Still, though, disagreement reigns about the content that fills in this picture.

The nineteenth-century French mathematician-cum-economist Antoine Augustin Cournot (1897 [1838]) was therefore by no means the first person to reflect on the way in which demand and supply might come together to produce the prevailing market price. However, he was the first to go beyond describing the outline of such a relationship in words to presenting the broad principle as a diagram. Cournot is not completely unknown to the economics textbooks, but where he is included there this is for the model that now bears his name, that of "Cournot competition" (Rivera-Batiz & Oliva 2003). This is an **oligopoly** model in which two firms compete over the quantity of a homogeneous product that they supply to the market, with every increase in quantity supplied helping them to make more profits. Having constructed a profit function for each firm Cournot was able to show, using the mathematical technique of partial differentiation, that there was a single point at which this competition would cease. This is where each firm's best response to the other firm's given level of output produces a solution where neither has an incentive to change its output levels (Kreps & Scheinkman 1988). This is a simultaneous solution of intersecting best responses that is easily captured using partial differential techniques. It could also be represented visually using demand curves for each firm within the same two-dimensional space.

Cournot's original use of demand-and-supply diagrams is weighted heavily in this way to first specifying in visual terms the mathematical underpinnings of market demand (J. Klein 1995). It would be to overstate the case to say that it was an afterthought to bring demand and supply together in a way that is so routine today. Yet it nonetheless remains the case that most attention in his 1838 *Recherches sur les Principes Mathématiques de la Théorie des Richesses* was focused on attempts to take the mathematical specification of market demand to a new level of sophistication. He was the first person to define the price-related properties of the demand curve in such a way whereby it could be presented visually as a downward-sloping curve (Blaug

1996). Everything else in this whole tradition of thinking follows from this one core innovation. On this basis alone, it is difficult to take issue with Steven Pressman's (2014: 57) surprise that Cournot's "reputation has not been much greater" amongst economists. Marshall himself could not have been clearer as to the focus of his intellectual debts. In private correspondence written in 1896, by which time his *Principles of Economics* was well established and all of its various applications of the demand-and-supply diagram were well known, he said the following: "as a fact my obligations are solely to Cournot" (cited in Dorfman 1941: 407). In the *Principles* itself, Marshall (2013 [1890]: xxii, 2013 [1890/1920]: 633) wrote of how his work was continually "[u]nder the guidance of Cournot", who he described in glowing terms as "a constructive thinker of the highest genius".

Although their visual representations of the market concept look much the same, one area in which Marshall's work differs from Cournot's is in the emphasis that can be found in *The Principles of Economics* on the condition of equilibrium. Viewed through the lens of the fully fleshed out analytical market concept, Marshall appears to have advanced on Cournot, because the classic demand-and-supply diagram bearing his name is used to socialize beginning economics students into thinking in terms of systems in equilibrium. However, Marshall was no more the originator of using the demand-and-supply diagram to study the stability properties associated with equilibrium points than he was of the demand-and-supply diagram itself. That honour goes to Karl Heinrich Rau in his 1841 *Grundsätze der Volkwirtschaftslehre*, in which he developed a rudimentary demand-and-supply diagram that he had first presented in a different publication earlier that same year (Rau 2016 [1841], 1841). At that time Rau might well have believed that he was the first to have experimented with the diagram and not merely the first to have seen the equilibrium applications to which it can be put. At the very least, all of the bibliographic evidence that has subsequently been unearthed suggests that Rau had no knowledge of Cournot's earlier work on related themes (Hennings 1979).

Like Cournot, Rau's use of the demand-and-supply diagram focused primarily on a specification of the demand side of the market. Rau investigated the special case where market supply is fixed at a constant level and displays no sensitivity to price whatsoever (Chipman 2014). However much the market price goes up this will still not be enough to tempt additional producers into the market. Visually this takes the shape of a vertical supply curve – as shown in Figure 4.2 – and it is a condition that the textbooks describe as perfect price **inelasticity** of supply. Rau asked what would happen if a product was priced too cheaply in such a market. He was able to show on his diagram that there would be excess demand at every price level below where the downward-sloping demand curve cuts the vertical supply curve. Rau worked

67

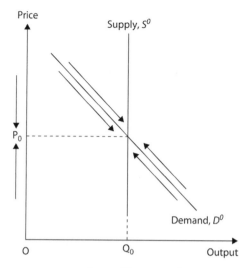

Figure 4.2: The movement towards equilibrium with Rau's vertical supply curve

through the possibility that producers would raise their asking price until a position was reached in which all of the excess demand had been eliminated. The same was true in reverse, whereby stocks of unsold goods would be accumulated if the price level was too high, prompting producers to lower the market price successively if they were to be focused on equilibrium. He even went as far as to express algebraically what the price adjustment would have to be until the point was reached where there would be no further tendency for price changes in either direction (Tribe 1988). This could be understood, he argued, as a function of the existing excess demand multiplied by the slope of the demand curve. Rau's demand-and-supply diagram therefore depicts the equilibrium point as some sort of price attractor. It is almost certainly with this image in mind that Samuelson chose to understand Smith's comment about the natural price acting as a gravitational force for market prices as a pre-emption of his own equilibrium scheme (see Chapter 2).

Exactly one hundred years after Rau's pioneering intervention, Samuelson (1941) cemented his own theoretical reputation by providing a more detailed mathematical exposition of how the equilibrium state arises from the progressive elimination of excess demand within the market (see F. Fisher 2003). By drawing the demand curve as a straight line this would mean that its slope in Rau's original formulation was the same under all conditions within his imaginary market. In this way the price change would merely be proportional to how far out of equilibrium the market was in the first place. Here we see the first visual representation of the market concept that presented the equilibrium condition as the underlying telos of market adjustment. Given the purpose to which this book has been written, we also see something else of interest. This was also the first time that the market concept was presented in a way that allows us to understand how easy it might be to start arguing that "the market" itself had a will of its own and was able to enforce an automatic price change that produced equilibrium.

Students will today be taught how the demand-and-supply diagram facilitates an analysis of economic welfare in a market setting (e.g., Johansson 1991; Little 2002). Aggregate welfare gains are always presented relative to the equilibrium condition, which once more makes it appear to be some sort of attractor. No student will be far into their introductory economics course before they will be expected to know how to reproduce the findings that show the way in which, at the equilibrium price, there will be both a **consumers' surplus** (reflecting the fact that some people would still have bought the product in question at a higher price) and a **producers' surplus** (reflecting the fact that some firms would still have been able to more than cover their costs at a lower price) (e.g., Katz & Rosen 1991). The first diagram in Figure 4.3 shows the shaded areas of consumers' and producers' surplus for a market with the equilibrium price P_0 and the equilibrium output Q_0. Every person on the market demand curve anywhere to the left of where the two curves intersect would have been willing to have paid more than the equilibrium price to take the product in question into their possession. The closer to the y-axis an individual consumer is positioned the more they save on the price they would have been willing to pay, and the greater the surplus they enjoy. The total consumers' surplus is denoted by the right-angled triangle AP_0B, formed by the y-axis, the line denoting the equilibrium price and the demand curve D^0. Equally, every firm on the market supply curve anywhere to the left of where the two curves intersect would have been

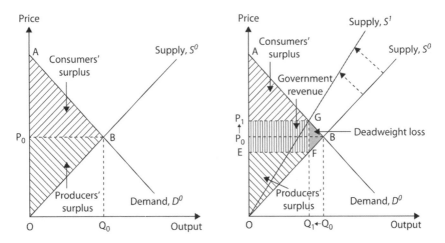

Figure 4.3: Diagrams showing consumers'/producers' surplus and the deadweight loss associated with a tax on production

able to have made the product more cheaply than the equilibrium price. The closer to the y-axis an individual producer is positioned the more they profit relative to their costs of production, and the greater the surplus they enjoy. The total producers' surplus is denoted by the right-angled triangle BP_0O, formed by the y-axis, the line denoting the equilibrium price and the supply curve S^0. The focus on surplus dynamics in turn enabled an analysis of the phenomenon that is now known as **price discrimination**, through which different customers are charged different prices for the same product commensurable with the price they are willing to pay.

None of these concepts were originally Marshall's. Those of consumers' surplus and price discrimination can be dated back to an 1844 article written by Jules Dupuit; those of producers' surplus and an enhanced understanding of consumers' surplus to three papers written between 1868 and 1872 by Fleeming Jenkin (Dupuit 1969 [1844]; Jenkin 2014 [1868], 2014 [1870], 2014 [1872]). Neither Dupuit nor Jenkin seems to have been familiar with the work of either Cournot or Rau (Humphrey 2010). This makes the elaboration of the market concept in its analytical form look like the fascinating scientific curiosity of multiple discovery (on which, see Lamb & Easton 1984).

Students will also learn from the demand-and-supply diagram what will happen when a government imposes taxes on either side of the market. They will be expected to know how to calculate the deadweight-loss effects on aggregate economic welfare that result when a tax restricts the overall size of market activity, as well as how to compare the **deadweight loss** to the revenue that the tax raises. Dupuit and Jenkin were once again the first to specify these consequences (Brownlie & Lloyd Prichard 1963). In the second diagram in Figure 4.3 we start again with a market in equilibrium with prevailing conditions P_0, Q_0 and with the consumers' and producers' surplus shaded on as before. The introduction of a tax levied on each unit of production this time shifts the supply curve to the left from S^0 to S^1. The overall surplus is reduced by the amount denoted by P_1GBFE, because the imposition of the tax forces the equilibrium price up from P_0 to P_1 and the equilibrium output down from Q_0 to Q_1. However, only a proportion of the foregone surplus, $EFGP_1$, becomes government revenue that can then be used to finance new public expenditures. The triangle BFG created by the new equilibrium output Q_1, the demand curve D^0 and the original supply curve S^0 is the surplus that is forever lost. This is the deadweight loss captured on the classic demand-and-supply diagram.

In the intervening period between the publications of Dupuit and Jenkin, Hans von Mangoldt (1995 [1863]) published his *Grundriss der Volkwirtschaftslehre* in 1863. It brought greater precision to the study of economic welfare by pioneering the technique of comparative static analysis that Marshall was later to make his own (Schneider 1960). At the hands of

Marshall's predecessors, the demand-and-supply diagram was used to provide a snapshot of multiple market conditions. The ingenuity of Cournot, Rau, Dupuit and Jenkin meant that all sorts of different market conditions were already a part of abstract economic theory. Nonetheless, this was still all about how a single market might be conceptualized in a single state. Mangoldt struck out beyond the others by showing what would happen when the underlying state of the world changes, represented by drawing on a new demand curve, a new supply curve, or both (Ekelund & Hébert 2014). Tastes and technology go alongside taxes as just three of the things that might cause the original positions of the curves to change.

DISAGREEMENTS AMONGST MARSHALL'S PREDECESSORS

"At any particular instant, the market price may not be the equilibrium price. If not, there will be either excess supply or excess demand, depending on whether the price lies above or below the equilibrium price. But these forces themselves provide the incentive to change prices towards the equilibrium price. In this sense, markets are self-correcting."

David Begg, Stanley Fischer and Rudiger Dornbusch, *Economics*

"[I]n a market system, if 'too much' of a commodity is being produced, its price falls; and if 'too little' is being produced, its price increases. The price remains stable only when a balance has been achieved between what producers are willing to produce and what consumers are willing to consume."

Michael Katz and Harvey Rosen, *Microeconomics*

From the foregoing, it would seem as though Joseph Schumpeter (2009 [1954]: 839–40) had every reason to wonder aloud in his magisterial *History of Economic Analysis* why his fellow economists insisted on viewing the Marshallian cross as the origins of the demand-and-supply tradition. He was equally adamant that it should be seen instead as its culmination. The question that must be asked in the context of this dispute is whether it matters who is right. Is there anything to be gained from substituting Schumpeter's preferred history of the demand-and-supply diagram for the conventional account that depicts Marshall as the trailblazer? My answer, unsurprisingly given the detail of the previous section, is "yes, it does matter" when the history of the demand-and-supply diagram is misremembered in this way. But this is where it is remembered at all. In the economics textbooks it tends just to be presented as is, without any attempt to colour in the backstory. On the whole they take all of the historical development out of the presentation of the demand-and-supply diagram, choosing instead to present the analytical market concept in recognisably Marshallian terms even when they do not associate Marshall's name directly with it. This suggests at least an implicit "no" to my question. It also suggests that all students need to know is the settled opinion today on how best to teach the demand-and-supply diagram, and if this means focusing specifically on the Marshallian variant then so be it. This in turn seems to be saying that there is no need to clutter students' minds with superfluous details about the tentative steps that were taken on the road to full elaboration of the demand-and-supply diagram: the priority should rather be becoming comfortable with the fully elaborated version. This, after all, is what Gregory Mankiw (2016: 20), the author of today's leading economics textbook, describes as "learning to think like an economist".

Appeals of this nature to an overwhelmingly instrumental pedagogical approach suggest that the market concept in its analytical phase abides rather strictly by the intellectual historian Stephen Stigler's (1980) somewhat tongue-in-cheek law of eponymy. This relates to the observation that it is much more likely for a scientific discovery to be named after the person who popularizes it and brings its many applications into the collective consciousness of the scientific community, rather than the person who initially reported the discovery. Perhaps it should come as no surprise that the most fundamental concept in economic theory should follow this pattern, as Stigler's father George once remarked that there are many instances in which early versions of a theory were not picked up because at the time the economics profession was simply not ready to be led in a new direction (G. Stigler 1982). In a much more pointed comment along similar lines, he also once reported agreement with a remark usually attributed in the original to Max Planck, which in his words became the observation that "a science progresses through the dying off of its old professors" (G. Stigler 1984: 311). The extent to which the work of Cournot and Rau remained unknown to the next generation of even like-minded economists in the 1860s plays up to this image of the analytical market concept as an idea whose time had not yet come. Marshall had a distinct advantage over Cournot and Rau in that he presented his version of the demand-and-supply diagram within a context in which his professional peers were willing to be persuaded.

It would be to belittle Marshall's achievements, however, merely to put them down to him being the right person in the right place at the right time. As Stigler – this time Stephen – points out, scientific laws are almost never named by historians of science so much as by practising scientists (S. Stigler 1980). In other words, the naming process is undertaken not by those people whose interest is in uncovering historical priority but by those who are conscious of the influence in their own theoretical work of the scientist who has been honoured with an eponymous law (Block 2012). The Marshallian cross diagram therefore became specifically the Marshallian cross diagram not because Marshall was the first to see its likely potential, but because he was the first to explain its full potential in a compelling manner to the whole of his peer group. It is a feature of Stigler's law of eponymy that the naming process reflects the general importance of the person who is immortalized in the name of the law rather than their specific contribution to how that law was revealed to the world (S. Stigler 1999). Although by no means universal, there was common recognition throughout the interwar period that economic theory, at least in its Anglophone version, was in a distinctly Marshallian phase (Shackle 1967). This was nowhere more apparent than in relation to the theory of the market in its partial equilibrium guise. As a consequence, there is maybe little reason to wonder why the most frequently used representational device for the market concept in that era should come to be linked quite so resolutely to Marshall's name.

Be that as it may, with one of the primary objectives of this book being to understand how the market concept has become so ubiquitous both in economic theory and everyday life, we overlook the disagreements between Marshall and his predecessors at our peril. But even the word "disagreement" might be a bit of a misnomer, because it is not as if there was an active debate between them. Marshall simply took what he wanted, repurposed it to his own design and ignored the rest. His predecessors' work in economics had long since come to an end by the time the *Principles* was well established, and so they were in no position to stake the claim that the differences in their approach led to a superior way of thinking. Moreover, it is the similarities between the early uses of the demand-and-supply diagram that have garnered most attention, not their differences. These similarities make it relatively easy to assume that all of the multiple discoverers were seeking to do essentially the same thing. The longer the passage of time during which Marshall's approach has been taught as *the* way to reveal the secrets contained within the demand-and-supply diagram, the greater the hold that this impression is likely to impart. Not only were Marshall's predecessors trying to do the same thing, this suggests, but more specifically they were trying to do the same thing *as* Marshall. However, my argument is that this risks diverting the focus from what remain very consequential differences between the earliest demand-and-supply diagrams. It also robs Marshall's specific presentational style of its contingency, making it easier to jump to the erroneous conclusion that what we mean by demand-and-supply dynamics presents itself to everyone in exactly the same way.

Most crucially, even when the diagrams are redrawn so that they all look the same, this does not mean that they all carry the same implied economic meaning. Today it is standard practice to draw the demand-and-supply diagram with the vertical axis labelled "price" and the horizontal axis labelled "output". Law's (1750 [1705]) very early eighteenth-century innovation in talking about "quantity and demand" has therefore by no means been expunged, because the "price" and "output" axes are today used to explore basic demand relationships relative to quantity. But "price" always goes on the vertical axis and "output" always on the horizontal axis. This is the convention into which economics students are always socialized. However, it is equally conventional in mathematics to place the dependent variable on the vertical axis. This, though, is not what Marshall did. When economics textbooks today teach the Marshallian cross diagram as the origins of mathematically-minded economic theory, they follow Marshall's economics convention in ignoring the mathematics convention. Marshall described the economic process of equilibrium determination in terms of output adjustments to prevailing demand and supply prices (Whitaker 1982). Output is therefore the dependent variable in the Marshallian world, with price the independent variable, but he placed his independent variable on the vertical axis of the demand-and-supply diagram and his dependent variable on the horizontal axis. This appears somewhat curious for someone sufficiently gifted as a mathematician to have been the second wrangler of his cohort in the Cambridge mathematics tripos.

Certainly it is not a feature of the work of all of Marshall's predecessors, who were all also highly skilled in the mathematics of their day. The classic demand-and-supply diagram entered the Anglophone economics literature via Jenkin, and he could not have been clearer that it was price and not output that he considered to be the dependent variable (Morgan 2012). When Jenkin's analysis is represented using Marshall's depiction of the diagram, visually there is nothing to separate their work. However, the eyes can deceive. What looks identical actually masks a very important difference in economic commentary. Marshall wrote about an economic process in which the quantity of a product in circulation adjusted to the difference between what consumers were prepared to pay for that product and what producers felt they needed to ask for it if they were to remain going concerns. The economic process that Jenkin sought to describe, by contrast, focused on price adjustments rather than output adjustments. Market-clearing potentials in his world are a function of price dynamics.

It might be worthwhile to pause for a moment to think about what this means in terms of the everyday language that ascribes to "the market" autonomous status as an actor in its own right. Price-adjusting market models make it seem very much as though it is "the market" itself that enforces the process through which disequilibrium might become equilibrium. Actual economic agents – i.e., those people who make decisions about the size of production runs and about how enticing a product is at its current price level – appear to be relegated to mere bystanders. It is "the market" itself that appears as though it is able to force the adjustment in price that is necessary if the point of equilibrium is ever to be reached. Look very closely at the economics textbooks and it will quickly become clear that the presentation of the Marshallian cross diagram is typically accompanied by an explanation of what is happening behind the diagram that more often than not focuses on the process of price adjustment. Despite their incommensurability because they exist on different ontological planes, these textbook accounts appear to feed directly into at least implicit support for the political idea that "the market" will always find the right price level if it is left alone to perform this task. Somewhat confusingly perhaps, this means that the Marshallian cross diagram can look indisputably Marshallian within the textbooks' visual representation, but, nonetheless, at the same time be surrounded by economic commentary that is equally distinctly non-Marshallian in its emphasis on price rather than output adjustment.

Such commentary owes much more to Cournot's theory, even if Cournot remains invisible in the explanation. The very earliest uses of the demand-and-supply diagram had the objective of understanding the difference between output-adjusting and price-adjusting market models. Such a difference is not merely one of implied economic content of the adjustment process. It also has implications for the scope of application of the market concept. Marshall's partial equilibrium models appear to work well in their own terms when talking about output adjustment in one market for one product. Attempts to specify the conditions of general equilibrium, however, have tended to proceed from the assumption that the relevant economic process is one of price adjustment. As will be explained more fully in the following chapter, the general equilibrium approach began with the work of Léon Walras in the 1870s. As such, it was already an active part of economic theory before Marshall presented what he believed to be the definitive account of partial equilibrium in 1890. Walras therefore could not have drawn for inspiration upon Marshall's work and its emphasis on the economic process of output adjustment. Instead, in his ground-breaking *Éléments d'Économie Politique Pure* he cited Cournot explicitly as a major influence and constructed his general equilibrium approach on the foundations of Cournot's model of price adjustment. Just to make it absolutely clear that he considered Cournot to have the sole right to scientific priority in this regard, he reminded his readers in the preface to the fourth edition of the *Éléments* in 1900 that "I have publicly acknowledged this fact in my first essays and on every suitable occasion ever since" (Walras 2003 [1900]: 37). However, in another apparent instance of Stigler's law of eponymy, it is usual today to refer specifically to Walrasian price adjustment to distinguish it economically from Marshallian output adjustment. Cournot thus appears to have been doubly overlooked in the process of eponymy through which economic theories are named.

CONTROVERSIES SURROUNDING THE DIAGRAM'S UNDERPINNING BEHAVIOURAL ASSUMPTIONS

"The assumption [of *homo economicus* suggests], most of all, that no one ever does anything primarily out of concern for others; that whatever one does, one is only trying to get something out of it for oneself. In common English, there is a word for this attitude. It's called 'cynicism'. Most of us try to avoid people who take it too much to heart. In economics, apparently, they call it 'science.'"

David Graeber, anthropologist and anarchist activist

"Could it be, I wonder, that there is such a thing as a wantologist, someone we can hire to figure out what we want? Have I arrived at some final telling moment in my research on outsourcing intimate parts of our lives, or at the absurdist edge of the market frontier?"

Arlie Russell Hochschild, Professor of Sociology, University of California, Berkeley

Despite the differences between the early accounts of the demand-and-supply diagram, they also have a number of common features that mark out this way of thinking relative to all previous iterations of the market concept. Pride of place in this regard must go to its underlying mathematization. It was impossible to successfully mathematize the market concept in its descriptive form, as has been discovered by those, like Samuelson, who have attempted to do so on the basis of the subsequent development of the market concept in its analytical form. There really does seem to have been a step change between Smith and Marshall. Of course, this difference is most pronounced when placing the two concepts side by side and paying no regard to what happened between their originating moments. Placing their developments back in real time, though, suggests more a series of incremental shifts in economists' theoretical instincts. Once the first tentative steps were taken towards the introduction of the language of "demand and supply", it became increasingly possible for economists to begin thinking in mathematical terms. And once the demand-and-supply diagram was firmly established, it became second nature for economists to treat their demand and supply curves like they would any other mathematical functions. Indeed, in many of the earliest uses of the demand-and-supply diagram it makes its appearance only after the relationship between demand and supply has first been described algebraically.

To express the character of demand and supply curves mathematically, however, changes the nature of the agents who can populate economic theories. The economic agents who appear in the descriptive market concept are allowed to retain all of their intrinsically human characteristics, including their flaws and frailties (Shapiro 2002). They are complex entities who do not necessarily follow any given template when thinking through alternative courses of action (V. Brown 1994). They might well have some sort of guide insofar as the moral norms of society will provide at least a degree of awareness about where the dividing line is to be drawn between appropriate and inappropriate behaviour. Yet it was a major claim of Smith's moral theory that only in exceptional circumstances would it be likely for anyone to constitute themselves as the ideal moral agent (Vivenza 2001). The dividing line between what people should and should not do might therefore be positioned differently in the minds of different people. This applied to decisions that they might take in the economic realm every bit as much as in any other sphere of life. In Smith's hands, then, the market concept is to be utilized in contexts in which there are distinct limits to agential predictability. Indeed, he put it to work in descriptive terms precisely to understand what might be necessary for two counterparties to agree to an exchange if that exchange was not to inflict harm on either of them. He might very well have been responsible for first using the noun couplet of "demand and supply" in a proto-modern sense, but his market concept made no behavioural assumptions that would render demand and supply mathematically tractable. It remained much too "real world" for that.

Cournot (1897 [1838]: 49–50, emphases in original), by contrast, began his account of the demand curve by saying that he wanted to express it mathematically and that, to do so, he needed to assume that it took on the properties of a "*continuous* function, *i.e.* a function which does not pass suddenly from one value to another, but which takes in passing all intermediate values". If you can imagine the way that it is conventionally drawn in the textbooks as a single line, this provides the most straightforward way of understanding what a **continuous function** looks like when represented geometrically in two-dimensional form. It passes through all transitional points in moving from one value to the next. Because of this, Cournot immediately spotted a restriction that he would have to impose on his market concept if his demand curve was to remain mathematically tractable as a continuous function. "It might be otherwise", he wrote in understated manner, "if the number of consumers were very limited" (Cournot 1897 [1838]: 50). If there were too few consumers on the demand side of the market, then a small group of them might be able to exercise sufficient influence on the structure of market pricing as to make the demand curve jump from one value to another. In the most extreme case a single consumer acting individually is all that is necessary to enforce such discontinuities.

Cournot (1897 [1838]: 50) therefore said that there would need to be a large number of consumers to protect the integrity of his demand-and-supply diagram: "the wider the market extends, and the more the combinations of needs, of fortunes, or even of caprices, are varied among consumers, the closer the function $F(p)$ will come to varying with p [price] in a continuous manner". Given the way in which the mathematics of continuous functions has evolved since the 1830s, it is now much more usual to begin by assuming the exact opposite of Cournot's concerns relating to a limited number of consumers. In a famous paper published in 1964, Robert Aumann (1964: 39) drew a direct analogy between "the continuum of points on a line ... [and] ... a continuum of traders" to say that the basic market model would work best if it was assumed that all markets were populated by an infinite number of consumers. "Very succinctly", he continued, "the reason for this is that one can integrate over a continuum, and changing the integrand at a single point does not affect the value of the integral, that is, the actions of a single individual are negligible". This leads to the most general theoretical findings possible, because guided by the mathematics every economic agent becomes a carbon copy of all others and no single person is distinguishable from anyone else in the independent effects that they can have on the prevailing price level.

The controversial element of this construction is not so much in the mathematics itself, because there is simply no other way to give a continuous function the generality that mathematicians so crave. If the classic demand-and-supply diagram is to offer insights into the condition of equilibrium that are to be mathematically meaningful, then it is a necessity to disqualify agential diversity of response in the face of behavioural norms. Anything other than the strictest condition of predictability will corrupt the mathematical result. Unless the objective is to create a wholly non-mathematical economic theory, then alternatives are very thin on the ground. The controversy arises in the next step, in the translation from a mathematical to an economic claim, where an infinite number of identikit agents in mathematical terms becomes a similarly infinite number of identikit agents in economic terms. It is not necessary to engage in any form of systematic empirical analysis to be aware that not all people think the same way, understand their desires the same way or wish to act the same way, let alone have the resources and capacities to allow their thoughts about wants to be manifested in action in the same way. A combination of common observation and an awareness of the impact of social structures is sufficient to confirm all this. Yet right from its earliest uses the demand-and-supply diagram has been founded on exactly such an assumption. The mathematics of "demand and supply" therefore takes precedence over the economics of demand and supply in economic theory. This is true even for Marshall, despite his famous methodological commitment to expressing theoretical claims in words not formulae, hence relegating the mathematics, at best, to a footnote (see Marshall 2013 [1890]: xxiii). Even here the words betray the constitutive influence of a distinctly mathematical logic.

Because it is so wedded to mathematical logic, the analytical market concept places very exacting demands on its economic agents. It expects them to have developed such a rarefied level of consciousness that they are attentive to every possible signal emerging out of the price system and never fail to align these cues to what is best for them personally in purely instrumental terms. The image of an abstract **homo economicus** thus looms large. However, this view of the human agent is actually distinctly non-human in its underlying orientation. It infers calculative capabilities that are more readily associated with a high-powered computer, and it also infers a willingness to ignore other people's interests that is similarly machine-like in its ability to be unmoved by emotions. Cournot had a somewhat "softer" description than this of what was required of his economic agents if the demand-and-supply diagram was to offer up mathematically tractable results. "We shall invoke but a single axiom," he wrote, "or, if you prefer, make but a single hypothesis, *i.e.* that each one works to derive the greatest possible value from his goods or his labour" (Cournot 1897 [1838]: 44). However, by the time that the late nineteenth-century marginalists had fully developed the idea that the equilibrium price is that which brings the very last consumer and the very last producer to the market, this assumption had significantly hardened. It was henceforward to be the case that economic agents were to dismiss every behavioural option that did not involve maximizing on the margin. Jevons (2013 [1871]: xxviii) wrote of economic theory subsequently encapsulating "a Calculus of Pleasure and Pain" through which everyone will be out to do the best solely for themselves. The mathematics of the demand-and-supply diagram would apparently not permit anything else. It thus appears that economic agents are reduced to acting out an economic logic that operates behind their backs. Indeed, more precisely, the economic theory requires them to act out a mathematical logic dressed up in economic clothes, and needless to say this too operates behind their backs.

Cournot appears to have offered a pre-emptive solution to this problem. He had evidently not yet made a complete break with earlier treatments of the market concept, writing that there were "many moral causes capable of neither enumeration nor measurement" that affect how economic agents might understand what counts as a fair exchange. We could have been transported right back to Smith's outline of the descriptive market concept in this comment. "Observation", he continued, "must therefore be depended on for furnishing the means of drawing up between proper limits a table of the corresponding values of D [demand] and p [price]" (Cournot 1897 [1838]: 47). This is an idea that Cournot came back to at the end of his famous chapter, "Of the Law of Demand", just in case any of his readers were guilty of missing it the first time around. "The construction of a table," he concluded, "where these values [of demand and price] could be found, would be the work best calculated for preparing for the practical and rigorous solution of questions" that are raised by the demand-and-supply diagram (Cournot 1897 [1838]: 53).

It is an idea that also proved to be tenacious. Jevons's (2013 [1871/1888]: 49) formulation in 1871 of demand curves by means of **utility** functions implied the use of observational data that might allow for the position and shape of the demand curves to be drawn in an empirically robust manner. He might well have thought that economic theory should subsequently focus on the hedonistic calculus, but he also assumed that a rethink would be in order if observational data pointed in a different direction to the theoretical conclusions. Edgeworth (2003 [1881]: 98–102) went as far ten years later as to propose the invention of a **hedonimeter** that might be able to scan brain activities to measure utility at source. Before this is dismissed as a laughable suggestion, a new generation of neuroeconomists is today working on imaging techniques that might directly replicate what Edgeworth had in mind (Colander 2007: 216).

Once more, though, we see important divergences in the work of Marshall's predecessors. Jenkin took an altogether different turn to create a path that has subsequently proved to be the one that most economists have followed. There is no available evidence, remember, to suggest that Jenkin was aware of Cournot's work, and therefore his view of what lies hidden behind the demand curve is not a direct challenge to Cournot. But this perhaps only serves to make the difference between the two even more significant. Cournot thought that observation alone was necessary if demand curves were to be taken out of the purely hypothetical realm of economic theory and have genuine explanatory purchase in the real world, whereas Jenkin believed that empirical confirmation of the theoretical claims was unnecessary. Cournot pressed for an understanding of the demand curve that was objectively based and rooted in data, but Jenkin argued that the demand curve could have no tangible presence because it existed purely in the heads of economic agents. It was therefore subjectively based and escaped easy reduction to empirical data. "In a given market, on a given day," he wrote, "the elements of the demand and supply curves already exist in the minds of purchasers and sellers" (Jenkin 2014 [1870]: 88). The important point in this regard is not that economic agents can say, under questioning, how their preferences map on to various combinations of demand and price to enable a demand curve to be constructed. It is merely that they must have been conscious of holding a preference, whatever that was and however imperfectly it was formed in their heads, for them to have made their recent purchases.

Four generations later Samuelson made ostensibly the same case when outlining the famous "**revealed preference**" theorem that now typically bears his name, where we do not need to be aware of the contents of an economic agent's preferences to see how they are revealed in the act of making choices. The naming specifically as Samuelson's revealed preference theorem is perhaps another example of Stigler's law of eponymy, and it is interesting to note that no mention of Jenkin appears in Samuelson's article. However, the most important thing about Samuelson's theorem for current purposes is also arguably its most controversial feature. It cleanses the analytical market concept of all the social stimuli that are such a crucial aspect of the market concept in its descriptive form. This facilitates the completely indefensible assumption that the mere act of choosing demonstrates that the choice made was an optimizing one (Samuelson 1948b: 244). From this perspective economic behaviour can therefore be treated as if it is a simple reflection of pure economic theory: the theory tells us all we need to know about behaviour and bypasses the need for observation.

CONCLUSION

"Psychologists sometimes use a technique called 'word association' to learn more about their patients. The psychologist says a word, then the patient says the first word that comes into his or her head … If a psychologist ever happened to say 'supply' to an economist, the response would undoubtedly be 'demand'."

Roger Arnold, *Economics*

"At the root of everything is supply and demand. It is not at all far-fetched to think of these as basically human characteristics."

Arnold Harberger, *The Concise Encyclopedia of Economics*

This chapter has focused on the market concept in its analytical form, the form that most of the economics textbooks present as *the* definitive treatment. It is more than possible to get all the way to the end of an economics degree and not realize that there is more to the market concept than the classic account of the demand-and-supply diagram, the Marshallian cross diagram. This chapter, though, has attempted to place the diagram back in the historical time during which its most essential characteristics were struggled over. Undertaking such an exercise reveals something instructive.

It suggests that there were competing origins of the demand-and-supply diagram that certainly include Marshall's *Principles of Economics*, but they also stretch back in time a good five decades before the first publication of that book in 1890. Each of these early accounts implied their own path to the future, but not all were followed with the same gusto. Economists tend to adopt a rather Darwinian approach to their subject field, whereby its history can be told in convenient terms as a series of steps through which only the best theory survives. However, this will surely not do. The tendency for the textbooks to present a singular approach to demand-and-supply dynamics can be misleading in this regard. It suggests that one route out of the quagmire of multiple discoveries has been embraced to the exclusion of all others. Yet this sits uneasily alongside the fact that imprints of a variety of these originating analyses continue to surface within the contemporary literature. At least implicitly so, they remain points of departure for disputes over economic theory today.

This is important as more than a finding of intellectual history. It also cautions us to think how far we are willing to accept the universalizing claims that are made so often on behalf of the classic demand-and-supply diagram. This, to be clear one last time, is what appears in almost all of the subject field's textbooks as the essence of setting up any investigation into any aspect of social life in the way of the economist. Laying claim to being an economist and learning to express yourself instinctively through the demand-and-supply diagram are treated as two sides of the same coin. But always this is about *the* demand-and-supply diagram as if it is everywhere the same thing, thus revealing essential secrets of how to isolate the fundamentally economic component of all behaviour. How can this be the case, though, if there were multiple discoveries of related ways of thinking all jostling for representation in the same basic diagram? To lose sight of these differences is to wish into existence a homogeneity that was not present in the original articulations of the theory. Do we run the risk of seriously overstating the ability of the demand-and-supply diagram to capture essential economic truths if we choose to ignore the fact that throughout its history it has facilitated competing economic theories and competing practical insights? And in turn do we also run the risk of allowing the essentialization of the analytical market concept to usher in the political thingification of "the market"?

The only way to avoid such risks, I argue, is to accept that there are limits to viewing the analytical market concept as a discrete entity. It looks more that way when set in comparison to what preceded it. The descriptive market concept, in which the focus is on the type of exchange relation that must prevail if both parties to the exchange are to avoid harm, is obviously markedly distinct from the analytical market concept. However many different ways there might be to express mathematical derivations of demand and supply functions in a two-dimensional diagram, they are all going to be much more similar to one another than any of them is to the descriptive market concept. This does not mean by implication, though, that the differences that underpinned the multiple discoveries of the demand-and-supply diagram are without interest. What I hope to have shown is that whilst it makes sense to think of the differences between the market concept in its descriptive and analytical forms, we have to remain attentive to the fact that the analytical form exhibits considerable heterogeneity. The more sophisticated the understanding of historical origins of the demand-and-supply diagram, the more inescapable the conclusion that the market concept passes through many Mk 2 phases. Each of these has its own chronology and its own temporality.

The foundations of economic theory are typically taught today through a perspective that emphasizes **instrumental rationality**. Every economic agent shares the same instinct for maximizing on the margin consistent with accepting that there can be no encroachment on their self-interest. They consequently look very much like the agents who appear bereft of all social stimuli in Samuelson's revealed preference theorem. They take cultural ignorance to absurd lengths in their search for a realm in which they can conduct themselves as economic automata. The economic theory dictates how they must act and, often, the mathematical premises on which the theory is based dictate the precise form of those actions. However, not all of the routes from the historical origins of the demand-and-supply diagram necessarily converge at this point. Others allow their economic agents to be more genuinely human, insisting that observational data and not axiomatic assumption will be used to inform studies of decision-making behaviour. If the economics profession currently congregates around the former variant of the market concept in its analytical form, then this in itself has to be seen as a conscious choice.

When such a choice is made, it is usually on the grounds of mathematical tractability. The classic demand-and-supply diagram may not look overtly mathematical at first glance, but it takes the form it does in the textbooks because the welfare conditions of equilibrium and stability it espouses can be drawn onto the diagram according to the rules of basic geometry. They can also be transposed from geometric to algebraic form via a system of equations. Both of these are clearly mathematical expressions, and restrictive behavioural assumptions are normally condoned on the grounds of doing whatever is necessary to enhance the mathematical precision of the underlying model. However, if this is true of economic models of partial equilibrium, then presumably it has to be even more true of the increasingly mathematically taxing models of general equilibrium that have sprung up within the economics literature. This is the focus of the following chapter, as my attention moves to the formalist market concept.

CHAPTER 5

VECTORS OF MARKET-CLEARING PRICES
The Walrasian auctioneer

INTRODUCTION

> "The major driver of economics is the equilibrium approach."
>
> Kenneth Arrow, Nobel Laureate in Economics

> "The ability to work with systems of general equilibrium is perhaps one of the most important skills of the economist, a skill which he shares with many other scientists, but in which he has perhaps a certain comparative advantage."
>
> Kenneth Boulding, Past President of the American Economic Association

In the move between the analytical and the formalist phases of the market concept, the presentation becomes much more abstract and the argument more technical. It is also where an explicitly mathematical mindset very obviously takes over. It is not as though the analytical market concept lacks mathematical underpinnings, as is perhaps best illustrated by the fact that Alfred Marshall's predecessors tended to provide an algebraic account of market-clearing dynamics before subsequently representing those dynamics pictorially on the forerunners of what is now the classic demand-and-supply diagram. Yet largely at Marshall's inception the mathematics remained hidden from view (Hart 2012). Instead, the most common way of explaining the market concept in its second phase is using words to describe what the reader can see on the diagram. Becoming familiar with those words is what it takes to learn how to speak in an avowedly "economic" manner, and in this way it is made to look as if an economic logic exists prior to the underlying mathematical structure. In truth, though, this is actually the use of an economic logic to strategically redescribe in economic terms relationships that are already revealed by the underlying mathematical structure. It is as if an attempt is being made to mask how much of the analytical process is produced mathematically. As the market concept reaches its formalist phase all such pretence is dropped (Ackerman & Nadal 2004). This is economics for only the most mathematically gifted, whereby a training in economics, counter-intuitive though it surely sounds, might well be a disadvantage to the academic economist relative to a training in mathematics. Perhaps unsurprisingly in these circumstances, conventional teaching texts in economics venture only tentatively onto the territory occupied by the formalist market concept.

This particular market concept has provided economists with moments in which they could focus on issues of scientific priority in the same way as mathematicians do. That is, there are problems to be solved, and once the solution is comprehensively worked out there is no need to go back to square one again. The solution stands for all time and the theoretical realm in which subsequent research endeavours take place has changed irrevocably. The holy grail for the formalist market concept in this regard was the search for a system of equations that could replicate an economic system in which all markets are in equilibrium simultaneously. In the language that was used by economists working in this tradition, the hunt was on for the so-called existence conditions under which market-clearing dynamics work perfectly throughout the whole of the economic system (Düppe & Weintraub 2014). Economists have generally liked to talk about the difference between **first best** and **second best** (Lipsey & Lancaster 1956), but this can be seen as a first-best solution to outdo all other first-best solutions. It is a state where a pure economic realm has been imagined into being (Geanakoplos 2004). Or it would be but for the fact that it is a mathematical thought experiment that has no obvious connection to the real world of actually lived economic experiences other than through the professional convention of giving the core components of the mathematical structure economic-sounding names.

The relationship between the mathematical and the economic dimensions of the market concept is always something to be kept in mind. This was never more the case than in the desire to be the first to deliver the existence proof to demonstrate that a single vector of prices might be said to exist within which all markets perfectly match demand and supply at the same time. Scientific priority in this regard must go to a 1954 paper published in *Econometrica* by Kenneth Arrow and Gérard Debreu. Stigler's law of eponymy appears to fall down in this instance when the existence proof is described as the "Arrow–Debreu solution" and the abstract world to which it relates the "Arrow–Debreu economy". Arrow and Debreu (1954) were definitively the first to produce a fully-specified existence proof, and they can justifiably be viewed as trailblazers when it comes to constructing the mathematical framework from which the existence proof arose.

Arrow and Debreu only ever collaborated formally on one paper, but it is not difficult to see why there was an immediate intellectual connection between the two when their paths first crossed. Arrow (1987) might very well have cited **Alfred Tarski** as his mathematical inspiration and Debreu (1984) **Nicolas Bourbaki** as his. Yet the fact that both came to economics only once they had forged their academic identities relative to some of the most high-powered mathematicians of the day tells us much about the way they approached questions of economic theory. Arrow received his Bachelor's degree from the City College of New York in mathematics in 1940, whilst Debreu passed his Agrégation de Mathématiques examination at the École Normale Supérieure in Paris in 1945 (Beaud & Dostaler 1997). By that time, economics had moved on significantly since Marshall's arguments to confine the mathematics to footnotes, and in the same timeframe mathematics itself had experienced a period of unprecedented technical advance. Despite his position as second wrangler of the 1865 Cambridge cohort, Marshall's mathematical skills were rather limited compared with Arrow's and Debreu's.

Arrow held prestigious university positions at Stanford and Harvard, Debreu at Yale, where he even held a joint post across the economics and mathematics departments. However, it was the fact that they had both worked for the **Cowles Commission** early in their career that provided the immediate prelude to their work on the existence theorem for general equilibrium (Louçã 2007). This was at a time when the Commission was based in Chicago, before hostility to its avowedly mathematical approach from the Department of Economics at the University of Chicago persuaded the Cowles family to move the whole operation to Yale in 1955 (Christ 1994). Eleven Nobel Laureates in economics have been recognized for the work they undertook at Cowles. That work is required in some way to reflect the Commission's motto, "Theory and Measurement", which in turn represents its commitment to bringing cutting-edge techniques of both mathematics and statistics to the visualization of economic problems (Erickson 2015). Both Arrow and Debreu were very much in the former camp of the mathematicians.

Indeed, so strong was their commitment in this regard that they could be said to have had one foot outside the Cowles tradition. The Commission's defining objective was always to be policy relevant, to produce economic models that would help policy-makers to target higher levels of overall economic welfare within society (Qin 2013). By contrast, Debreu (1991) was always adamant that his equations for general equilibrium held no such promise and that it was a mistake to believe that they applied to anything more "real" than the mathematical structure out of which they arose. Arrow was more sanguine about the potential practical application of his equations (Arrow & Hahn 1971), but he too always operated at a level of mathematical abstraction that was some way beyond the typical Cowles approach of using probabilistic models based on systems of simultaneous equations (see Westland 2015). Albeit suitably upgraded to incorporate contemporary technical developments, this looks like a reboot of the mathematical insights on which the earliest studies of general equilibrium were founded, whereas what Arrow and Debreu were attempting to do was to reset mathematical economics qualitatively anew.

However, just as Marshall had predecessors in relation to the demand-and-supply diagram, so too Arrow and Debreu followed in other people's footsteps when attempting to visualize the perfect market system that needed nothing other than demand-and-supply dynamics to produce coherent internal laws of motion. The whole general equilibrium tradition of thinking started with Léon Walras in the 1870s, and Arrow and Debreu's 1954 *Econometrica* article must be seen, therefore, as an end-point of four generations of scholarly effort. Walras (2003 [1900]: 37) set off with the express intention of restricting his system of equations to talking only about economic processes as they arose in real historical time. However, he failed to solve the so-called market coordination problem at this level. His successors moved closer to a solution through increasingly replacing the economic content of the underlying market concept with mathematical content (Nicola 2000). By the time of Arrow and Debreu's famous 1954 paper, it was hardly an exaggeration to say that the economic content had become a sideshow to the mathematical structure.

In an attempt to chart the significance of this shift to the changing nature of the market concept, this chapter now proceeds in three stages. In section one I look back to a time before Marshall's seminal presentation of the classic demand-and-supply diagram, to when Walras was initiating his own branch of the history of the market concept. There is no straightforward chronology in operation here, then, as the Mk 3 phase of the market concept had clearly been activated some time before the Mk 2 phase had been fully fleshed out. The analytical and formalist market concepts therefore overlap in time in interesting ways. However, Walras's account of the market concept only really reached full maturity after the classic demand-and-supply diagram had long been established as the primary visualization technique for what a market was in economic theory. The remaining sections look at what happened to the market concept once the existence proof that solved the market coordination problem had become an accepted part of economics. Section two charts the route from Walras to Arrow and Debreu's famous 1954 *Econometrica* article. This is the story of how high-powered mathematics increasingly displaced economic content within the existence proof of general equilibrium economics. Section three looks at the way in which some semblance of an economic process was maintained, but only ever by making that process less and less realistic.

WALRAS'S EARLY STUDIES OF GENERAL EQUILIBRIUM

"It took from a hundred to a hundred and fifty or two hundred years for the astronomy of Kepler to become the astronomy of Newton and Laplace, and for the mechanics of Galileo to become the mechanics of d'Alembert and Lagrange. On the other hand, less than a century has elapsed between the publication of Adam Smith's work and the contributions of Cournot, Gossen, Jevons, and myself."

Léon Walras, marginalist pioneer

" ... the unrealistic elements of the *tâtonnement* process. How can all the traders in the economy gather in one place and exchange tickets?"

Akira Takayama, *Mathematical Economics*

It must have been something of a shock to his fellow economists when they first found themselves trying to engage with Walras's 1874 *Éléments d'Économie Politique Pure*. This was not because there was anything particularly novel about his foundational assumption of what it was, at heart, that drove economic activity. He started, much as Carl Menger (1981 [1871]) had done three years earlier in his *Grundsätze der Volkswirtschaftslehre*, with a subjective theory of value. In this conception the value of a product is not tied to any of the intrinsic properties inscribed into it via the production process, but rather to how people register its "worth" personally to them. That worth, in turn, relates to how many other consumption possibilities they are willing to give up to make this one particular purchase. This whole way of thinking stretches back further than Menger, though, with Walras himself identifying it in the work of Menger's German-language predecessors, including some of the pre-Marshall pioneers of the demand-and-supply diagram (Mirowski 1984). There is a direct reference in the *Éléments*, for instance, to "Mangoldt's *supply and demand curves* which a number of English economists, following the lead of Mr. Marshall of Cambridge, are wont to employ", in a way that was not replicated in Marshall's own *Principles* (Walras 2003 [1874/1900]: 483, emphases in original).

It was also not Walras's mathematical instincts that would have come as a shock to readers being exposed to his work for the first time. Jevons noted immediately the similarity between Walras's *Éléments* and his own *Theory of Political Economy*, like Menger's *Grundsätze* also published three years previously in 1871 (Howey 1973: 22). Jevons (2013 [1879]: lxi) thought that they had both seen the same potential in using elementary calculus to determine the position of **turning points** in continuous consumption functions. These turning points were mathematically meaningful, because they made it possible to derive points of tangency where the slope of the consumption function was at either a maximum or a minimum point. It was also a relatively small step for both Jevons and Walras to translate the mathematically meaningful properties of a continuous consumption function into economically meaningful statements. Set within the marginalist assumption that the most relevant economic activity takes place "**on the margin**", using elementary calculus to determine turning points drew attention to the all-important last unit consumed, last unit produced, last unit exchanged, etc. The analytical market concept was thus still a feature of Jevons's and Walras's work, even if their mathematical instinct was to present the market concept algebraically through the use of differential calculus rather than pictorially via the demand-and-supply diagram.

What made Walras's work stand out was the sheer scale of the mathematical application and how that opened the door to an altogether different articulation of the market concept. Nothing like Walras's mathematical ambition had ever been seen before and he took the thought experiment surrounding the market concept into previously uncharted territory. Jevons and Menger were still using their marginalist techniques to discuss how demand-and-supply dynamics might operate in a single market considered in isolation. They were noticeably working within a tradition that Marshall described as partial equilibrium. Walras (2003 [1874/1900]: 126), by contrast, thought that the differential calculus could provide insights into how the process of price determination in one market might have an effect on multiple processes of price determination in other markets. In other words, the abstract principle that results in simultaneous price determination across the whole of the economy might possibly be revealed by the use of a system of simultaneous equations based on the differential calculus (Plantz 1964). This, of course, is a much more complicated application of mathematical instinct than that which underpins Jevons's *Theory of Political Economy*. It is impossible to escape the feeling when you open Walras's *Éléments* that, compared to anything else that had been written in economics at that time, you have just entered a more complex mathematical world. It reads as if it is placing more exacting mathematical demands on its audience, and it looks that way too. It consists of reams and reams of mathematical equations in an attempt to significantly scale up the scope of the underlying market concept.

As specialist Walras scholars have been eager to point out, however, just because he went further than anyone previously to mathematize the market coordination problem, this does not mean that he was *only* interested in the mathematical characteristics of hypothetical market-clearing dynamics (Van Daal & Jolink 1993). When he embarked on the first edition at least, he had the goal of placing the mathematics and the economics of the market coordination problem in direct conversation with one another. The mathematics was to be used to locate the argument at a sufficiently abstract level to make it possible to think in terms of simultaneous market-clearing dynamics, but this was not to be at the expense of being able to specify how markets might be said to clear in everyday economic life. In other words, he set off clear in his own mind that he wanted to do more than merely derive a system of equations that might have a single hypothetical price structure that allows demand to equate with supply in all markets (Bridel 2011).

"Merely" is perhaps the wrong word in this last sentence, because as future struggles for the existence proof of general equilibrium demonstrated, it was an outstanding intellectual achievement to get that far. Yet Walras's real interest was in the economic adjustment mechanisms through which prices moved iteratively towards the point of general equilibrium. He worked, remember, with the underlying notion of a price-adjusting economy, whereas Marshall always had in mind the idea of an output-adjusting economy (see Chapter 4). It therefore made sense to Walras to think in terms of prices that are anything but given and that instead experience movements reflecting economic decisions about how best to produce and how best to consume (Walras 2003 [1874/1900]: 147–8). Or it did for the first three editions of the *Éléments*, at which stage Walras was required to review how many "real" economic processes he would be able to allow into his theory. As so often seems to be the case, the decision to think again about his starting premises was driven by his increasing realization that it might be impossible to solve the market coordination problem solely as a matter of economics. The formalist market concept became increasingly mathematical in orientation, then, on the back of a failed endeavour (Turk 2016).

Walras began with the idea that the underlying price structure changes over time and that these changes are driven by real economic factors linked to technological advances, research and development expenditures and investment in the product life cycle (Collard 1973). Over the short term, however, producers do not have much latitude to alter their pre-set production runs. Demand-and-supply dynamics can only operate in contexts such as this through price changes leaving the impression that they are feeling their way towards an equilibrium position. He called this process "*tâtonnement*", a word that has its own distinct meaning in French but which is not easily translatable directly into English (Walras 2003 [1873/1900]: 170). Most historians of economic thought treat it as a means of capturing the sense in which the price mechanism departs a state of disequilibrium in the search for equilibrium, but is by no means guaranteed to get there in one go (Walker 1987). Exiting a state of disequilibrium might therefore only be to enter another, this time different state of disequilibrium. The hope, though, is that because the price mechanism has some sort of auto-corrective property, the passage through each successive stage of disequilibrium will be less prone to mistakes than the last when viewed through the lens of the equilibrium point. *Tâtonnement* is therefore the trial-and-error process through which the price mechanism "gropes" its way towards a structure of equilibrium prices (Currie & Steedman 1990).

It should be noted straightaway, though, that this conception of market-clearing price adjustments relies on treating the price mechanism as if it has a number of essentially human characteristics. The price mechanism itself becomes the agent in Walras's theoretical account. It has to be entrusted with the knowledge of where the equilibrium position is, and it is what sets in motion the process of eventually getting to that destination. Actual people are rather bypassed in the resulting exposition. However, this appears to run in diametrical opposition to Walras's stated aim to explain price adjustment in real historical time and as a real economic process. It is consumers whose decisions ultimately change the market's underlying demand conditions, and it is producers whose decisions ultimately change the market's underlying supply conditions. Yet these actual people have their agency transferred to the only ever abstract concept of the price mechanism in Walras's account. Today it is commonplace in political discourse to hear "the market" being talked about in agential terms, as something that is able to identify where its interests lie and to call upon the capacity to ensure that those interests are satisfied. There is a clear pre-emptive parallel here in Walras's conception of *tâtonnement*. "The market" is replaced by the price mechanism in being granted a will of its own as if it might be understood to take on a human form. But as the price mechanism is what drives all market dynamics in Walras's theory then this difference is really not very large.

The first three editions of Walras's *Éléments* therefore look like a far from perfect match for his stated objective of solving the market coordination problem in genuinely economic fashion. However, the fourth edition of 1900 completely gave up on approaching the problem in this way. The language of *tâtonnement* was retained in what is now generally considered to be the definitive version of the book, but in the actual act of producing equilibrium it is a *tâtonnement* process that seems to have had all of its groping eradicated. This makes a lack of direct translation from the French to the English all the more regrettable, because the word that is usually taken to refer to a trial-and-error process of groping now appears to have been used in an analytical context in which such a process is disqualified by definition. When Walras wrote about disequilibrium processes from the fourth edition onwards there was still a sense in which the market mechanism was feeling towards a necessarily indistinct future. However, when that future was rendered distinct by the use of the equilibrium concept, all intimations of a groping process were removed (Walker 2003). The equilibrium position was simply stated as being in existence, not explained economically in terms of a series of iterative moves towards it through real-time consumption and production decisions.

This does not help to clear up any residual confusion about the precise conditions that the market concept is supposed to be describing. Indeed, it almost certainly adds a new layer of uncertainty. In the fourth edition of the *Éléments* Walras used his *tâtonnement* concept within the context of a so-called **pledges model** (Mirowski & Cook 1990). This is a simplifying device that acknowledges the inherent difficulties of trying to theorize the incalculably high number of individual decisions that occur in an actual economy as they happened in real historical time. But what exactly is being pledged and when in Walras's famous pledges model?

Producers are required to make a written statement about how much market demand they will be able to cover in any given time period. In the original French, Walras (2003 [1874/1900]: 242) used the word "*bons*" to describe these pledges in a signal that producers would be good to their word when it came to their commitment to market supply. They could be trusted not to produce either a unit more or a unit less of their product than they had promised. It did not really matter, then, when they made their written pledge as long as it existed formally in writing, because it would lock them in to a given level of production for the entirety of the period under investigation. The commitment that Walras enforced on producers in his abstract world therefore acted as some sort of non-negotiable contract. This had the effect of fixing output throughout the process through which equilibrium was generated, because producers were not allowed to go back on their word even if remaining true to it meant operating a clearly dysfunctional business model. In this way, it looks as though Walras had introduced a neat conceptual trick for ensuring that equilibration relied on price-adjusting rather than output-adjusting dynamics, were it not for one other change between the first three and the fourth editions of the *Éléments*. This is that there was no *process* of equilibration left at all, because the concept of *tâtonnement* had been stripped of its dynamic tendencies when discussing specifically the condition of equilibrium.

As a consequence, Walras did not hold output constant so that he could get a better look at how prices would have to move over time if there was to be a situation in which more and more markets were brought into equilibrium. Instead, he used his pledges model merely as a device for arguing that a single structure of prices might be thought to exist that brings all markets into equilibrium simultaneously. In essence he gave up on trying to solve the market coordination problem as an explicitly economic matter. From the fourth edition of the *Éléments* onwards he broke all links between the economics of his theory and the economics of real-world adjustments so that the market coordination problem might be rendered solvable in mathematical terms. Others clearly followed in his footsteps (Guesnerie 2011). As the race gathered momentum to be the first to publish an existence proof of the condition of general equilibrium, it became clear that the economic content of the process of equilibration was of only limited significance to the main goal. We should therefore give serious consideration to the proposition that the formalist market concept is every bit as much a mathematical concept as an economic concept, even asking whether it remains an obviously economic concept at all.

THE ROAD TO ARROW AND DEBREU'S EXISTENCE THEOREM

"Mathematics is nothing more, nothing less, than the exact part of our thinking."

Luitzen Brouwer, Dutch mathematician and philosopher

"Nothing has done more to render modern economic theory a sterile and irrelevant exercise in autoeroticism than its practitioners' obsession with mathematical, general-equilibrium models."

Robert Higgs, economic historian

If Arrow should be considered an economist who was previously trained to an exceptionally high level in mathematics, it might be necessary to conclude that Debreu was primarily a mathematician who just so happened to venture into economic theory. They went their separate ways after their one and only collaboration for the famous 1954 *Econometrica* article, content not to join forces again so that they could each follow their own chosen path out of the existence proof (Horn 2009). Arrow remained forever intrigued by the thought that genuine economic meaning could be extracted from the mathematical structure of the general equilibrium model. His intention therefore seems to be to bring his work fully into line with the Cowles Commission's ultimate objective of informing welfare-enhancing policy decisions (Arrow 1973). He returned to those equations time and again in attempts to push the existence proof into further areas of enquiry that would reveal something new about the economic secrets that lay locked up within the market concept. Debreu, by contrast, thought that the existence proof provided a purely mathematical solution to a purely mathematical problem and that this was the only type of problem to which the 1954 paper could speak (Debreu 1987). He was consequently not tempted to return to the existence proof in the search for hidden economic meaning within its structure, because he believed that the process of inferring such meaning represented a jump in meaning that the mathematical structure of the proof on its own did not permit. Once he had helped to solve the market coordination problem mathematically his instincts told him that this was a case of job done and that it was time to find another mathematical problem to occupy his thoughts. It really was not his thing to spend too much time wondering how best to refine policy so that it might create a space for enlarging the economic welfare gains to be shared across society (Debreu 1986). It is perhaps no surprise from this perspective that, when Debreu gave the obligatory press interviews when learning that he was to receive the 1983 Nobel Memorial Prize for Economic Sciences, he sounded as if he was trying to accept the award as a mathematician (Düppe 2012a).

The separate trajectories on which Arrow and Debreu set off mirrored an important methodological divide that Walras outlined in the *Éléments*. He distinguished between the ability to demonstrate findings in relation to the market coordination problem "in principle" and "in effect" (Walras 2003 [1874/1900]: 242). Walras's development of the market concept proceeded in the first instance on the basis of demonstrating the logical possibility of a structure of prices that not only leaves every single market in equilibrium but the whole market system too. This is a demonstration "in principle", and for Walras it meant immersion in specifically mathematical argumentation. Such a step had to be completed, he believed, before it was possible to ask the most obvious subsidiary question of whether a reasonable facsimile of the conditions that solve the market coordination problem "in principle" is able to be found in the economy in which everyday life is conducted in all of its complexity and contestability. This would be to show how markets replicate the structure of general equilibrium "in effect". There are two ways of interpreting the change in meaning of the *tâtonnement* concepts between editions three and four of Walras's *Éléments*. The first is that by de-emphasizing the demonstration of market coordination "in effect" he was simply recognizing that this was personally beyond him and he would have to leave it to others. The second is the rather bigger claim that he had experienced a moment of epiphany in which it dawned on him that it was entirely impossible to solve the market coordination problem "in effect".

There is nothing in Debreu's research that contradicts this second reading of Walras's apparent change of heart. After all, he was adamant that work conducted at the mathematical level could only speak to mathematical problems (Debreu 1984). This can be seen as an outright denial of Walras's two-step approach. If you were to ask a question that might only be answered in abstract mathematical terms, Debreu seems to have been implying, then you can only possibly be working with demonstration effects that operate "in principle" (see Punzo 1991). There is no admissible route in such circumstances from "in principle" to "in effect". Debreu's relationship to Walras might therefore be seen only in relation to deepening the older man's "in principle" findings. Walras's mathematical argument came to a halt with saying that a solution to the market coordination problem was logically achievable, but Debreu was able to show what it was. Arrow, meanwhile, and at least compared to Debreu, appears to have been more of a methodological as well as a theoretical devotee of Walras. He searched extensively for the bridges that might connect general equilibrium findings "in principle" and "in effect" (Arrow 1987). The search for extractable economic meaning from the existence proof implies as much. However, that search was hardly a ringing success. As Frank Hahn (1973a), one of Arrow's later collaborators, has argued, most of the economic findings to have arisen from research in the general equilibrium tradition have been strictly in the negative. That is, they show what *cannot* be deduced economically from the market concept in its formalist phase, rather than what can be (Rizvi 2003).

The debate about how far the market concept should be mathematized is therefore an important one. The proponents of this approach suggest that mathematical abstraction provides a neutral language that allows the properties of market relations to be appraised by the standards of logic alone (Dow 2016). In other words it enables a pure market essence to be distilled in a way that is uncorrupted by political distortions (Benetti, Nadal & Salas 2004). The separation between what belongs in the purely hypothetical realm of economic theory and what belongs in the real world could hardly be clearer than it is in this instance. Markets are never anything other than political in the real world, because the introduction of market institutions in place of something else necessarily entails new distributional consequences (e.g., Cohen 1995; Miller 1999; Galbraith 2002). The language of "the market" is no less inherently political, because it is used in an attempt to naturalize market institutions and therefore close off the space for discussing non-market distributional settlements. Yet the proponents of a highly mathematized market concept make their case on the basis of assuming that to render that concept using ordinary language is to run the risk of missing some of its essential features because of the intrusion of an unwelcome political dimension into its development. It is difficult to see the market concept for what it truly is, so the argument goes, if the discussion quickly descends into a debate about how far market institutions should be allowed to encroach into social life.

However, this was *precisely* the question that Walras (2003 [1900]: 40) thought his work on the market coordination problem obliged economists to ask (see also Kolm 1968). And what of Arrow, who, as a closer replica of a true Cowlesman than Debreu, followed Walras's methodology in trying to take the demonstration of general equilibrium from "in principle" to "in effect"? He also thought that the derivation of greater knowledge about the acceptable limits of market institutions in social life was the only reason to want to study the market coordination problem in the first place (Arrow 1983). Hahn (1973b) took a very similar position. To the argument that mathematics cleanses the market concept of unhelpful political distractions, these leading mathematical economists were happy to endorse the counter-proposition that the market concept will always remain necessarily political.

The distinction between a purely mathematical and a genuinely economic rendering of the market concept is relatively easily explained by looking at how the route to Arrow and Debreu's existence proof relates back to Walras's initial investigations into the conditions of general equilibrium. The story of the existence proof is often told as if it represents the heroic scientist changing the world by plucking a brand new finding out of thin air (Krauss & Johnson 2009). After all, correspondence between the journal's editors has subsequently come to light that shows how their search for an economist with the mathematical skills to confirm the validity of Arrow and Debreu's model proved utterly fruitless. Their *Econometrica* article therefore had to be accepted every bit as much on trust as by the normal academic standard of peer review (Weintraub & Gayer 2001: 434). Yet still it is necessary to acknowledge that it did not emerge out of nowhere so much as being the culmination of a collective search undertaken by a group of dogged and brilliant researchers. They were admittedly small in number and they stood so at odds with what was considered mainstream economics at the time that there is a definite subterranean feel to their work. But they were nonetheless a marked presence on the margins of mainstream debates.

The mathematical construction that did most to take them out of the shadows and propel them to the centre of subsequent theoretical discussions was the **fixed-point theorem**. This was a theorem that had yet to be adequately fleshed out in Walras's day, but was available to Arrow's and Debreu's most immediate predecessors. If the search for the single structure of prices that might clear all markets simultaneously was to have a direct mathematical analogue, then the similarly singular structure of the fixed-point theorem presented itself as a plausible candidate. But note that this can never amount to more than argument through analogy, which means that the analysis must stop with Walras's "in principle" condition. Building a general equilibrium model on the basis of the mathematical construction of a fixed-point theorem can show us what the relevant structure of prices would look like were it to be a perfect approximation of that mathematical construction. Yet it cannot tell us how sensible it is to assume that there is anything within the actual economy that might produce a price structure of this nature.

The fixed-point theorem that has exerted most influence on economists' theories of the market is the one that was first fully elaborated by Luitzen Brouwer in 1909. Brouwer in turn was building on Henri Poincaré's research on the so-called "**three-body problem**" (Barrow-Green 1997). This problem became a central focus of nineteenth-century mathematical enquiry into the stability of objects in the solar system: how might it be possible to work out the respective motions of, say, the Sun, the Earth and the Moon simply from knowledge of their positions, masses and velocities at a particular moment in time. Poincaré showed that it was impossible to stipulate the trajectory of motion for any more than two bodies using the prevailing techniques of differential calculus (Szebehely 1967). Some other technique therefore had to be developed to permit the mathematically interesting scaling up of a solution to the three-body problem into a solution to an n-body problem.

Poincaré believed that the answer he was looking for related to the topological properties of the area in which the motion of the three bodies took place (Mawhin 2005). If a number of restrictions on the shape of that area were to be allowed, he demonstrated that the trajectory begins to approximate a limit cycle (Hirsch & Smale 1974). Nobody went further in the early twentieth century than Brouwer in successfully generalizing Poincaré's findings (van Dalen 2013). Brouwer was fascinated by all matters topological and began work on a generalized proof of a fixed-point theorem on the back of Poincaré's following observation. However vigorously you apply yourself to stirring a cup of coffee, there will always appear to be a point that remains still, where to the human eye at least no motion is visible. Providing the topological conditions are right, this point can then be used as the baseline for facilitating the calculations to solve the n-body problem. Brouwer (1911) eventually managed to extend this basic intuition into a generalized theorem stating that for any continuous function f that maps a compact convex set into itself there has to be a point x_o such that $f(x_o) = x_o$. x_o is the fabled fixed point.

It can be described mathematically as such, but it still does not guarantee that any easy route is available for calling to mind what this fixed point might look like in a pictorial representation (see Chapter 2). The equals sign in Brouwer's equation suggests that the fixed point can be "seen" by the highly mathematically-trained eye, but it is a completely different matter to be able to see it in terms of its underlying physical properties so that it might be drawn onto the sort of diagram that is routinely used in economics. Because of this, a giant leap of the imagination was required at the time to deduce the relevance of Brouwer's work for economists' theory of the market. Yet in retrospect it is not hard to understand its appeal. Walras's glorious failure when setting out to solve the market coordination problem economically using differential calculus took on a different complexion as soon as it became known that Poincaré had shown that differential calculus was inadequate to solving any variant of the three-body problem. Clearly a general equilibrium model can never hope to bridge the gap to an "in effect" demonstration if the number of markets it is able to talk about is such that $n<3$. There are evidently many more markets in the real world than this.

Yet this in turn means that Walras had equipped himself with the wrong mathematics for the task at hand. Or perhaps it is more accurate to say that the right mathematics for what he was trying to do was simply not available to him, whatever his skills as a mathematician. He could ask the wonderfully provocative question of what it would take to imagine an economic system where the interconnections between each of its individual markets lined up so perfectly that demand equated with supply in every one of them all at the same time. But he could not show the form that the prevailing structure of prices would have to take if his hypothetical economic system was to reveal a solution, because his use of differential calculus placed this objective forever out of reach. Brouwer's fixed-point theorem, by contrast, held out renewed hope for success amongst those who followed in Walras's footsteps. For a start, the use of Brouwer's fixed-point theorem meant that n could be as large as you wanted it to be when solving the n-body problem, which mapped nicely on to the observation that the number of markets in existence in everyday life is far too big to count. Moreover, the definition of equilibrium provided by economics textbooks both past and present is that it is a state of the world from which there is no tendency to change. It is a fixed point, in other words, departure from which necessarily involves a reduction in economic welfare. What better way might there be of investigating the properties of this fixed point than through a fixed-point theorem? Equally, though, what more needs to be said about the loss of economic content when the market concept is constituted through mathematical analogy in this way?

THE ECONOMICS OF THE FORMALIST MARKET CONCEPT

"I've never known an auctioneer to lie unless it was absolutely necessary."

Josh Billings, nineteenth-century humourist

"Auctioneer, n. The man who proclaims with a hammer that he has picked a pocket with his tongue."

Ambrose Bierce, nineteenth-century wit

Arrow praised Walras for having seen the ouline of a theory whose time, in his day, was yet to come. Even though Brouwer had fleshed out the first iteration of his famous theorem only a year before Walras's death, Arrow believed that Walras had nonetheless really been talking the language of a fixed-point theorem all along (Weintraub 1985). This might just have been an act of intellectual generosity on Arrow's part, designed to ensure that Walras continued to be credited on matters of scientific priority. Whatever the real reason, though, it should be clear that the path from Walras to Arrow and Debreu's *Econometrica* article was actually much more elongated than this. Their eventual existence proof exhibits the influence of John von Neumann's pioneering work on game theory in the 1920s, Abraham Wald's proto-existence proofs in the 1930s, Shizuo Kakutani's development of Brouwer's fixed-point theorem in the 1940s and John Nash's equilibrium theory of non-cooperative games published in 1950 (Ingrao & Israel 1990). Besides, the text of the *Éléments* does nothing to support the supposition that Walras was only trying to solve the market coordination problem by mathematical analogy. There should be little doubt that what he really wanted to do was to show how the unique structure of prices consistent with general equilibrium was generated economically (Walras 2003 [1900]: 40). Indeed, the lengths to which he was prepared to go to stipulate a genuinely economic transmission mechanism in the fourth edition of the *Éléments* is all the proof that is needed that his genuinely economic ambitions in the first edition never really deserted him.

It is necessary to revisit his pledges model to see exactly what was involved. By requiring all producers to remain true to the level of production they had promised to supply to the market, Walras had discovered an ingenious way of holding output constant. All of the focus could thereby be concentrated on price adjusting market dynamics. Yet it is a distinctive feature of the later Walras's work that no such adjustment occurs. To think in terms of adjustment requires the structure of prices that solves the market coordination problem to arise iteratively over time. From the fourth edition of the *Éléments* onwards, Walras allowed the temporal dimension across which his abstract economic system operated to be entirely dissolved into a single moment. At that moment a single structure of prices was cried out. Moreover, it was not any old structure of prices, so much as the one structure that cleared all known markets simultaneously and that hence solved the market coordination problem. This single cry was heard throughout the economy and acted as some sort of starting gun (Watson 2005b). It was the moment that producers began to act on their pledges of how much they would supply to the market, and because all in-time real historical dynamics had been eliminated it was also the moment at which production was required to cease. The same was true of all consumption too, which also had to begin and end in the same instant.

There is a single character, then, who is responsible for ensuring the condition of general equilibrium. The whole point of the market coordination problem is to show how decentralized decision-making in the context of numerous decision-makers and myriad economic decisions appears to produce coherent outcomes. Yet the device that Walras inserted into his later theory for crying out the correct structure of prices altogether goes against the presumption of decentralized decision-making and myriad economic decisions. There is only one decision of note here – regarding the precise content of the structure of prices that must be internalized throughout the economy in the same instant – and even then it is not what happens economically that determines the equilibrium structure of prices but rather what has to happen if the mathematics is to work properly. The single decision-maker must therefore be gifted a profound degree of knowledge, being capable of evaluating every pledge across the whole of the economy and being able to predict how those pledges relate to every conceivable level of market demand. It is not without reason that the Walras scholar William Jaffé (1967: 2) called the character in question "a computer-like *intellectus angelicus*".

Others have asked themselves which other character from economic theory it most resembles and have chosen to call it instead the "auctioneer" (F. Fisher 1987). This is one instance in which Stigler's law of eponymy does not really seem to apply when it gets named more specifically the Walrasian auctioneer. Even though he did not give it this name himself, nobody before Walras had seen the requirement for such a character to make their market concept work. No economic activity can take place in Walras's mature theory in the absence of the auctioneer carrying out its one prescribed role of announcing the structure of prices that clears the entire market system. However, it is required to occupy the curious dual position of being at once embedded right at the very heart of the economy but also being at one stage removed from it. The auctioneer necessarily has to be an element of the market system if it is to be an effective carrier of all information that impacts upon the condition of general equilibrium. Yet at the same time it must also necessarily exist apart from the market system because it has to remain unmoved in the face of the distributional consequences of market outcomes. Walras thus appears – at least on this issue – to have pre-emptively accepted Debreu's subsequent claim that the mathematics of general equilibrium has to stand alone in its own terms, but without ever throwing his hat fully in with the mathematicians. The language of the auctioneer is certainly not a straightforward mathematical language, yet to what extent can it be considered a self-evidently economic language either, seeing as it creates an insuperable obstacle on the path from demonstrating general equilibrium "in principle" to demonstrating it "in effect"?

An auctioneer construct is also entirely necessary to Arrow and Debreu's existence proof. There are two very different ways of looking at whether or not this is unexpected. On the one hand, it might appear to be so, given the respective levels of mathematical skill displayed by first Walras and then Arrow and Debreu. This difference is more than a function of time, despite the vast array of advances that occurred in mathematics in the eighty years between their core treatises. It is also a function of raw capability, because Arrow and Debreu significantly outperform Walras on any reasonable test of mathematical potential. It might well raise some degree of surprise, then, that the same purely fictitious character that had to be relied upon for Walras to assert that market-clearing conditions had been met also reappeared in Arrow and Debreu's work. No mathematical analogy that got closer to describing actual market processes was forthcoming in the interim. On the other hand, we might not be surprised by this at all if it is the case that Walras's failures were actually an indication that there simply is no economic solution to the market coordination problem and that something akin to the auctioneer construct will always be necessary if the impression of such a solution is to be maintained. This might merely be a conceptual trick to enable the mathematical solution to be passed off as an economic solution, but Walras should be credited with a great deal of foresight if his initial embrace of it was evidence that all other routes to a genuinely economic solution were unavailable. His failure might therefore be repositioned as a "failure" (with obligatory inverted commas) if true success was unattainable. After all, if economists with the mathematical skills of Arrow and Debreu were unable to push the underlying mathematical analogy any further in the direction of genuine economic meaning, then who could be expected to do so?

It was not as if Arrow and Debreu had not discussed the possibility of removing the auctioneer construct in conversations about earlier drafts of what eventually became the famous 1954 *Econometrica* article. Debreu's concern that they had not been able to eliminate the auctioneer had been his "most important criticism" of where he thought the paper was heading (cited in Düppe 2012b: 483). Yet its published version nonetheless references the crucial role played in their theory of market coordination by "a fictitious participant who chooses prices, and who may be termed the market participant" (Arrow & Debreu 1954: 274). Needless to say, the market participant is given the ability to choose the one structure of prices from which a solution to the market coordination problem emerges out of the system of equations that describes the hypothetical economy under investigation. No real choices are being made by anyone else who might be assumed to act within this economy, because they are required to be purely passive receptors of the equilibrium structure of prices.

The topological surface that Arrow and Debreu model as an economy allows for an infinite number of markets both now and in the future. In other words, it covers every possible product that might be bought and sold today and every possible product that might be bought and sold at any possible time to come. However, no actual buying and selling takes place, at least not in the conventional sense of monetary purchases (Tabb 1999). Arrow and Debreu present an infinitely repeatable auction as their conception of the economic system, but it is an auction that is condensed into a single instance on the basis of perfect barter (Rogers 1989). There is no second auction because there does not need to be one if the auctioneer has already cried out the structure of prices that allows everyone to barter their way to the general equilibrium solution. Equally, though, as nobody is given a chance to change their mind or correct their earlier errors, it is difficult to believe that they are exhibiting any real choice. Their decision-making capabilities are reduced to slavishly following the implications of the single structure of prices that proves that the fictional auctioneer has done its job.

What are we to make, then, of the fact that in its formalist phase the market concept permits only a single decision-maker who stands in for the whole of society? More pointedly perhaps, what can we say about the identity of this single decision-maker? Who is it? The existing literature provides us with three possible interpretations.

The first of these makes no compromise at all on the suggestion that such a highly mathematized account can only ever exist within a purely hypothetical realm. That is, it argues that the economic system that delivers results consistent with perfect market coordination can only ever be the product of human imagination. For sure, it requires an imagination so creative that the publication of Arrow and Debreu's existence proof remains a eureka moment that continues to astound and thrill in equal measure. But it is also the case that it is the economic theorist alone who has enforced the condition of general equilibrium. This condition has nothing to do with the internal economic dynamics of the theoretical system under investigation. The auctioneer construct is doing the bidding of the theorist who has set off with the express intention of demonstrating that the general equilibrium solution exists. Every decision about how economic agency is to be enacted is therefore in the gift of the theorist. Robert Clower (1995: 314) has gone as far as to argue, in consequence, that "the notion that the analysis deals with anything 'decentralized' is an abuse of language". This suggests instead that all decision-making is concentrated in the hands of the person who has brought the general equilibrium model to life on the page (Udehn 1996). The auctioneer construct is thus the personification of the wishes of the theorist.

The second interpretation makes much more of a concession to the idea that relationships in the theorists' self-made abstract world might still be replicated to some degree in the real world. However, the restricted scope of application of this translation between the two worlds still suggests that it is hardly an unequivocal advance on what has gone before. The auctioneer construct becomes somehow "real" in this second interpretation if it can be assumed that a single person populates the whole of the market environment on behalf of everyone within society. That person can therefore see what is needed to hold a structure of preferences that maps on perfectly to the structure of prices that the auctioneer already knows will lead every market to clear simultaneously. This is the so-called "**representative individual**", whose preferences are a perfect microcosm of society's in its entirety and who allows the process of market coordination to only have to deal with one set of producer preferences and one set of consumer preferences (DeCanio 2014). However, the representative individual can only act in this way if it has a particular combination of character traits imposed upon it. If the representative individual is to stand in for society in a way that matches the aspirations of the auctioneer, it must be laser-focused on denying any impulses to action that are not of the strictly utility-maximizing variety. In other words, it has to be the ideal manifestation of the *homo economicus* we met in the previous chapter (Kirman 1989, 1992). Despite the increasing mathematical sophistication of the formalist market concept, then, on this issue it is indistinguishable from the analytical market concept.

The third interpretation makes no distinction between the auctioneer construct and the market environment in which it is supposed to operate. It thus neatly sidesteps the confusion that arises from having to presume that the auctioneer is simultaneously both internal and external to the market by arguing that this is the wrong way of looking at the question. If the auctioneer is necessary for solving the market coordination problem but that solution is to be attributed to the inherent superiority of market institutions, then why not simply assume that the auctioneer and the market are one and the same entity? After all, Walras's initial specification of the *tâtonnement* process was designed to show the way in which the market mechanism gropes its way to equilibrium. All studies subsequent to Walras's fourth edition of the *Éléments* have done away with the conception of groping in favour of an auctioneer construct that solves the market coordination problem in one shot. But even though the market mechanism no longer gropes its way to equilibrium it is still the market mechanism that is responsible for the production of equilibrium. However, this merely reignites the problem of treating "the market" as if it was an agent embodied with human capabilities to think, aspire and act for itself. It is to provide an abstract conceptual construction with the will to break those bounds and to impose its interests on to actual human agents.

CONCLUSION

> "In recent years, the meaning of the term *equilibrium* has changed so dramatically that a theorist of the 1930s would not recognize it."
>
> Robert Lucas and Thomas Sargent, Nobel Laureates in Economics, "After Keynesian Macroeconomics"

> "God does arithmetic."
>
> Karl Friedrich Gauss, German mathematician

The history of the market concept in its formalist phase looks different to the history of the market concept in its analytical phase. The classic demand-and-supply diagram that denotes the analytical phase, at the superficial level, was all about multiple discoveries of ostensibly the same thing. As shown in the prevous chapter, however, at a deeper level it was about a plurality of ways of capturing the internal economic dynamics of market adjustment, thus giving a lie to the claim that this was actually all the same thing. There is a degree of diversity there that typically goes unremarked upon when the beginning economics student is told how markets work. This is a case of many people seeing the same thing, at most, in *largely* the same way, but where the difference in the details is still highly consequential. By contrast, the history of the formalist market concept is much more about a single problem being posed and then the incremental moves that took place over time to solve it. This difference perhaps merely highlights how these two accounts of the market concept diverge on the issue of technique. Yet in both instances it is necessary to ask how much of the explanation is located at the level of economic process and how much at the level of mathematical expedience. Each will be presented against the backdrop of a clearly specified economic problem and will be discussed, at least in summary form, in clearly articulated economic language. Equally, though, each will allow for a number of restrictions to be introduced for the ease of mathematical modelling, even if this makes the ensuing argument less realistic in economic terms.

Nowhere in economics has argument by mathematical analogy been pushed further than in the search for a solution to the market coordination problem. Walras had described the basic properties of a general equilibrium economic system in what, for his day, looked to be exceptionally sophisticated mathematical terms. In truth, though, this was merely the first step in the process through which mathematicians took over the elucidation of economists' central concept. It bears repeating that when Arrow and Debreu finally unveiled their existence proof in 1954 there were not enough sufficiently mathematically trained economists to check that there were no flaws in their mathematical reasoning (Weintraub & Gayer 2001). The market concept was therefore being driven to a level of abstraction that made it unfamiliar in its formal presentation even to those who we might expect to have known it best. It requires top-end mathematical skill to be able to call to mind the vectors of market-clearing prices that dominate the Arrow–Debreu world.

As was the case with the previous two chapters, the intellectual history in this chapter has been introduced for reasons that go beyond purely historical curiosity. It is important to understand what the market concept has been deprived of in the move towards mathematical formalism. The thought experiments that such a move have facilitated have led to achievements that are never less than seriously impressive in their own terms. Yet they do also come at a cost. They have placed the market concept in a realm in which the decisions of actual people have no bearing on the discussion. It is difficult to imagine even the most automated markets in real life being propelled by anything other than human volition, but the mathematical logic embedded in the formalist market concept takes this human dimension away. Walras might well have had no intention of producing an agent-free market concept, and an economist as mathematically talented as Arrow attempted to put some sense of human agency back into it. But the result has nonetheless been to move the market concept ever further away from the study of real-time interpersonal relationships that marked it out in its descriptive phase.

This has been controversial in itself, but it is made doubly so when we recall just how much it narrows the number of participants who can express themselves through this particular version of the market concept. The vast majority of economists are excluded on the grounds of the mathematical demands that it places upon them, let alone the vast majority of non-economists. The latter group is left to find some other way of talking about market relations in a context in which refinements to the market concept often imply that it has auto-corrective properties. There remains a significant gap between the market concept and market ideology, but all talk of auto-corrective properties still helps to sustain the image of "the market" as something that controls its own destiny. This second image is much more widely accessible. It requires no top-end mathematical skill; indeed, no mathematical skill at all. It relies only on being tuned in to the way in which political debate has been structured over the last forty years or so. What remains intensely unfamiliar at one level immediately becomes much more familiar at another, because a life governed by the realities of "the market" is the life that so many of us have grown up being told that we will lead. The final substantive chapter will now explore the rhetorical devices through which this account of "the market" has taken on a number of the properties of a contemporary common sense.

CHAPTER 6

THE POLITICAL RHETORIC OF "THE MARKET"

INTRODUCTION

> "Pareto optimality … is an economic state where resources are allocated in the most efficient manner."
>
> www.investopedia.com

> "A society can be Pareto optimal and still perfectly disgusting."
>
> Amartya Sen, Nobel Laureate in Economics

It is hopefully clear by now that "the market" is not something that can do anything to us of its own volition. It is not an essential being; it has no innate force that demands obedience; it does not ask us to think carefully about our preferences or tell us that we must satisfy its interests; it plays no active role in our lives in and of itself. It really is not a thing to which agential characteristics might be ascribed. And yet this is still the most likely image that is being created when appeal is made politically to "the market". There remains, then, a tension between the market understood conceptually and "the market" understood ideologically. The absence or the presence of the inverted commas still does make a big difference. The objective of the final substantive chapter is to explore the extent to which this gap remains fundamentally unbridgeable by seeking to learn more about the political rhetoric of "the market" and how it is not always clear whether that rhetoric is being applied to something that most obviously reflects the conceptual or the ideological use of the word.

If the market concept as developed in economic theory provides no basis for saying that "the market" is something that does anything to anyone, there must still be something in it that has allowed this idea to become so prevalent. There might remain a jump, a big jump even, between the market concept and market ideology, but that jump must still appear to be navigable to at least some degree if market ideology is to resonate with people's sense of what is going on in their everyday lives. That is, there might still be aspects of the market concept that anchor the images that are transmitted through the use of market ideology. It is very difficult to think that this something, whatever it is, relates to the descriptive market concept, where the market is understood as a physical marketplace with all the attendant personal interactions that bring such physical spaces to life in human experiences. The search must therefore be restricted to the market concept in its analytical and formalist phases, where these human experiences disappear in deference to the search for an essential underlying economic logic. The phrase "the market" is often used as shorthand for some such logic.

The most important element of the market concept in this regard is the idea of equilibrium. This is both only ever a logical property in its own right and also one of the key sources of the misinvocation of the logic of "the market". In an important sense, the thingified form of "the market" is merely the extension of the thingified form of the concept of equilibrium. Of course, nobody could ever be expected to recognize if a point of equilibrium had actually been reached and demand in the real world matched supply in the real world, for the simple reason that this is purely an abstraction drawn from theorists' self-made world and makes sense in its own terms only there. It has no clear real-world counterpart. Rhetorically, though, the very idea of equilibrium is rich in symbolism. It translates in theoretical terms to the point at which all potential welfare gains within the economic system are exhausted. Any factor that intervenes to move the hypothetical economy away from equilibrium therefore necessarily incurs a welfare loss. If the equilibrium point is one that cannot be improved upon within the theoretical model then it is relatively easy to see how the view might develop that it is also one that should be targeted in practice.

It is commonly assumed that it is "the market" itself that produces equilibrium, or at the very least the pricing dynamics of market institutions perform that feat. Set in this context, the otherwise large jump between the market concept and market ideology maybe reduces to a rather smaller jump (smaller in rhetorical terms, that is, if not necessarily in ontological terms). If equilibrium is the desired point and "the market" is the mechanism for producing it, then "the market" comes across as something that should be nurtured into existence where it does not already exist, as well as secured from outside interference where it does. This still is not the same as saying that "the market" is exerting its own will over us, but it does lead to a similar conclusion that it is the ultimate arbiter of what is a good and what is a bad economic decision.

In this construction, it is only "the market" that has the foresight to know where the equilibrium position is and the knowledge to implement the economic structure that is consistent with equilibrium. Any other position preferred by any other actor must necessarily be inferior to the equilibrium position preferred by "the market" and must thus also necessarily give way to it. Workers will not want to see their jobs outsourced because their firm moves part of its operations to where labour is cheaper. Consumers will not want to see their living standards squeezed because increases in commodity prices mean that it is harder to make ends meet. Producers will not want to see a loss of market share because a competitor has been the first to successfully harness a new technological development. In all three instances these people will experience disturbance to their own personal equilibrium, because, they are told, it is predestined that the equilibrium of "the market" will win out. A similar argument can be made if you think back to the three examples with which the book began. If there is a common denominator in Mitterrand's failed experiment in what became known as "Keynesianism in one country", East Asian countries' inability to reproduce their previously successful pegged exchange rate regime and Bear Stearns's implosion under a financial house of cards created out of mortgage-backed securities, then it is this. In each instance the ostensible corrective applied by "the market" was one that is commonly understood to have involved it imposing its preferred vision of equilibrium.

In an attempt to show how a pervasive and powerful rhetorical structure has developed in support of this view of "the market", the chapter now proceeds in three stages. In section one I highlight recent arguments suggesting that "the market" has gone beyond the point of reification to that of deification. In other words, it is now no longer treated just as a thing so much as a thing with divine features. In section two I show that this is entirely consistent with a trend towards creating automatic pilots for managing the economy so that the ultimate place at which the policy decision is made is at least one stage removed from democratic control. Such outcomes might be thought of as being part of a trend towards depoliticization, but they are no less political in essence for having had their actual politics increasingly removed from view. When "the market" is treated as a thing then this can easily lead to depoliticized policy outputs, and when it is treated as a thing with divine features then this rhetorical structure almost always resonates even more potently. In section three I seek to look behind the veil of the rhetorical structure to ask what exactly is being taken out of view when appeals are made routinely in this way to "the market". It is surely ironic that in as many instances as not these appeals mask a structure of decision-making that is the complete antithesis of what is conventionally assumed to be a free market economy.

THE DEIFICATION OF "THE MARKET"

> "We have created new idols. The worship of the ancient calf has returned in ... the idolatry of money. In this system ... whatever is fragile, like the environment, is defenceless before the interests of a deified market."
>
> Jorge Mario Bergoglio, Pope Francis

> "From the intrinsic evidence of his creation, the Great Architect of the Universe now begins to appear as a pure mathematician."
>
> Sir James Hopwood Jeans, English physicist, astronomer and mathematician

It is far from a recent phenomenon that those whose political preference is for as much "market" as possible to express their faith in decentralized economic institutions to get the job done. "The market" is not only something to be trusted, but something where the trust borders on the reverential. Just as with respect for religious norms, respect for decentralized economic norms is to be increasingly unquestioning, where the status of the messenger is such that the message is always to be taken as it is. For forty years and more now, a new breed of market fundamentalist has happily referred to itself as believers, true believers even (Block & Somers 2014). A game of outbidding one another often ensues, through which a struggle takes place to demonstrate who is the purest devotee of the creed.

However, there is still something distinctive about more recent appeals to believer status. It is entirely possible to make it clear to anyone who is prepared to listen that you believe instinctively in the ability of decentralized economic institutions to always produce the best possible solution – in short, that "the market" always knows best – without at the same time investing those institutions with god-like properties. There are two very different ways, then, in which faith in "the market" might be proclaimed. To get from the generic sense of an insightful, knowledgeable "market" to bestowing the qualities of a divinity upon it involves yet another rhetorical jump. It is, of course, some such jump in the first place to ascribe any sort of agential characteristics to "the market" and to argue that it is able to impose its own will on proceedings. As I have argued throughout the book, this is to attempt to render "the market" through a human essence. It is another step altogether, though, to claim that the will in operation is specifically divine. Deification of "the market" out-trumps reification of "the market" because the human essence is replaced by something very similar but that transcends the strictly human and takes us into the heavenly realm. In this way "the market" becomes an avatar in the theological meaning of the word.

Viewed from the perspective of the previous substantive chapters, in which I have focused primarily on the development of a number of different accounts of the market concept, this all looks distinctly odd. How could a concept that arises from within a strictly hypothetical realm in which the emphasis is placed on the economic condition of matching demand with supply suddenly become infused with the imagery of an individual being required to match themselves to the teaching of religious authority? These would seem to be entirely parallel abstract worlds offering no scope for inter-section or overlap whatsoever. Perhaps again, though, the idea of equilibrium is the source of all of the action, rhetorically speaking at least. How might market institutions be expected to produce such a pristine condition as equi-librium, one in which no more welfare gains are possible for society as a whole, if they are to be limited to the realm of the human?

The move between the analytical and formalist phases of the market con-cept might be particularly important in this regard. Alighting on equilibrium in a single market is impressive enough on its own. It requires the coordina-tion of many optimizing consumption and production schedules but in the absence of a formal enforcement mechanism to undertake the coordination. This is a spectacular success to be attributed to "the market". But think how much more spectacular the success becomes when we are talking about not a single price that clears a single market at a single moment in time so much as a vector of prices that clears all conceivable markets at all conceivable moments of time. Is there any wonder that such a market system might be viewed as having its origins in something divine?

Yet it must be remembered that the idea of equilibrium exists solely within economists' self-made abstract world (Samuels 2007). It is a concep-tual abstraction that makes sense in its own terms within that world, but which does not translate easily beyond it into anything that we could go out and actively explore in empirical terms in the real world (Tieben 2012). The question of whether "the market" has a human essence or divine properties is therefore entirely moot. It has neither, not in any real sense in any case. The emphasis on purely hypothetical conditions of equilibrium is enough on its own to show that the market concept exists at the level of thought experiment. To get from there to positive endorsements of market ideology by those who are confirmed believers in the creed once again brings us to the requirement to jump from one register to another.

However, this is where things can quickly start to get complicated by the fact that when we hear the single word "market" it can be unclear which var-iant of the market concept is in play and therefore a number of very different images might be called to mind. It is, in general, only the analytical and for-malist market concepts that permit the replacement of the human essence of "the market" with something that has god-like properties, because it is only analytical market concepts that contain the ostensibly divine condition of equilibrium. The more mathematical the analytical market concept the more straightforward it seems to be to make a move of this nature. It has been a commonplace of intellectual history, after all, to conflate the mathematical and the divine, to treat the most impressive mathematical achievements as if they were blessed with divine beauty (Koetsier & Bergmans 2005). The descriptive concept of the market as marketplace seems relatively immune to such a conflation by comparison, because it simply does not exist at the right level of abstraction for this transposition to be enacted. An added complication arises here, though, because it nonetheless remains the case that marketplaces developed historically around physical sites that were set aside specifically for the purpose of worship. The Christian church, perhaps in particular, often shared spaces with the commercial centre of the town, with the two frequently boasting shared architectural forms in which the reflection of one echoed through the other (Giggie & Winston 2002).

As Stefano D'Amico (2012) has shown in relation to Milan, arguably the best example of the dual construction of Christian church and secular market, the city was laid out specifically so that religious and commercial activities could occur side by side. The famous Piazza del Duomo consequently enlisted a use of space that served two masters at once. Yet the boundaries between the two uses were hardly drawn rigidly. The commercial sides of the piazza were arranged in individual shops that gained authority in the minds of economic agents as legitimate places to buy and sell because of the way that they mimicked in material form the side chapels of the cathedral that were separated from one another so that each could be dedicated to its own saint (Stabel 2008). The shopkeepers appealed to religious imagery as a means of effecting spiritual as well as economic interest in their products, thus bringing the feel of the cathedral, if not literally the cathedral itself, into their commercial smallholdings. Moreover, economic activity also extended into the cathedral, but this time literally, with sewing, weaving, stonemasonry and fruit selling all taking place on the floor of the church (Watkin 2005). Perhaps this was only to be expected, though, as the institution that oversaw the cathedral throughout its construction phase, the Veneranda Fabbrica della Duomo, had set itself up with a secure means of future income by also owning the surrounding market structures (D'Amico 2012).

Each town and each city will have its own tale to tell about the way in which its religious and commercial activities were constituted in spatial terms. However, it is by no means the exception for the history of the production of urban space to reveal a very close connection between the two. Religion and commerce might very well conventionally be seen as competing sources of social authority, and when appeals are made to Friedrich Nietzsche's idea of the death of God then it is usually in the context of the rise of a supervening commercial logic (Bulhof & ten Kate 2000; Kirby 2000; Bayman 2001). Surely it is more than coincidence that Nietzsche had a madman announce that God is dead specifically within the town's marketplace. The void that is left behind when a society of non-believers no longer relies on religion to anchor their lives has no more appropriate setting in Nietzsche's mind than the physical meeting place through which people seek metaphysical meaning in buying and selling activities. "The market" is responsible for killing God in this view of events, or at the very least the responsibility falls on those who allow themselves to be so readily seduced by market ideology. Surely it is also more than coincidence that Nietzsche (2006 [1882]: 90, emphases in original) had the madman say specifically to a group of market traders in response to his question of "Where is God gone?": "*We have killed him – you and I!* We are all his murderers." The marketplace therefore looks to be the ideal location for proclaiming that, for many people, market ideology has been able to replace religious devotion as the most likely meaning-making device in everyday life. The irony is surely not lost that this is despite the fact that marketplaces were often only built in the first instance by the same people that built places of worship.

A double irony might be entailed if, in Nietzsche's reading, it was "the market" that supplanted various gods in society's affections but now, in contemporary political rhetoric, it is also "the market" that has led to a rejuvenation of faith in something divine. It is necessary to issue a reminder straightaway that this rejuvenation involves a series of often undefended moves between three different variants of the market concept and their transposition into political rhetoric via the process of thingification. But these are still connections that are worth exploring. Rhetorically at least, "the market" as some sort of divine essence represents the world that so many of us are required to live in today. Nobody has described the appeal to something divine in this rhetorical phenomenon more thoroughly or more compellingly than the theologian Harvey Cox in his 2016 book, *The Market as God.* He has shown how Christian theology reaches its most deferential plateau when ascribing to an unseen deity three interlocking "omnis": that it is omnipotent, omniscient and omnipresent. The divine spirit, in other words, is all-powerful, all-knowing and everywhere ever-present. Cox (2016: 264–78) suggests that the same rhetorical features now propel a new market theology. This is quite some leap from exploring the purely hypothetical conditions of the concept of equilibrium.

The commitment to faith comes in when needing to be sure that omnipotence, omniscience and omnipresence are unquestionable attributes of divinity but without seeing direct evidence of the existence of a god on a daily basis. The true believer can have no doubt that their god is real, even if its transcendent qualities are visible in the words of the theologians but not to the eyes of mere mortals. "The market" might be said to be locked in to this same curious dualism in which the political theologians who extol its virtues describe its omnipotent, omniscient and omnipresent attributes, whilst the rest of us are left to wonder at what the "it" really is. We are not to try to second-guess what it wants, or so we are routinely told, because we will simply be subjected to corrective action that could be punitive in the extreme. Think Mitterrand; think Thailand; think Bear Stearns. As the famous saying goes, "the market" is not to be bucked. From this perspective, why would we ever want to try to second-guess it in any case, because no human actor has the ability to know what is best for them in the way that "the market" does? And with its reach increasingly extending into more and more areas of social life the refusenik option of attempting to create alternative institutional forms beyond its scope is getting progressively more difficult to activate (Lipschutz & Rowe 2005).

Ignoring for one moment that we are clearly back to the "it" problem outlined in the Introduction – i.e., of how "the market" can ever act in thingified form – contemporary political theologians have even armed themselves with a pre-emptive answer to the challenge of theodicy. Put simply, there might always be difficulties in keeping the believers believing if instead of benevolent design what their eyes are telling them they see is death, destruction and decay (Farley 1990). Why would a caring deity who is equipped with the awesome powers of the "omnis" allow such occurrences? The political theologians of "the market" have a straightforward answer that they have shown themselves to be only too happy to forward with increasing self-assurance over the last forty years or so (Shaanan 2017). However much "market" there currently is, they say, it is not enough. However frequently their political opponents point to instances of market failure, "the market" will only fail, they argue, when it is introduced in anything other than completely pristine form. Whatever anyone says about "too much market", they counter that there is too little, as well as that the continuing gap between market reality and market potential impedes the full realization of the "omnis". Cox (2016: 8) suggests that this maps almost perfectly on to the twentieth-century trend towards **process theology**, which posits the existence of a finite deity that is only ever moving towards the infinite position at which the three "omnis" emerge in truly unimpeded form. The deity is always in the process of becoming and therefore necessarily remains incomplete (Suchocki 1989), just as the political theologians tell us about "the market". The deity also has to be continuously struggled over so that it is defended against the sceptic's view that all sorts of socially regrettable outcomes count against its very existence (Cobb 2016). Once more the rhetoric of the political theologians operates on exactly the same plane of justification.

THE AUTOMATIC PILOTS OF "THE MARKET"

"The stampede toward 'rational expectations' ... derailed the expectations-driven model building that had just left the station. In the end, this way of modeling has not illuminated how the world economy works."

Edmund Phelps, Nobel Laureate in Economics

"Most mainstream macroeconomic theoretical innovations since the 1970s [especially the rational expectations revolution] ... have turned out to be self-referential, inward-looking distractions at best. Research tended to be motivated by the internal logic, intellectual sunk capital and esthetic puzzles of established research programmes rather than by a powerful desire to understand how the economy works – let alone how the economy works during times of stress and financial instability."

Willem Buiter, Chief Economist at Citigroup

Cox (2016: 211–14) argues that the political theology of "the market" now possesses its own scripture, its own liturgy and an in-depth account of how human sin prevents pristine market institutions from always revealing themselves in their true colours. Any attempt to temper what "the market" might otherwise be able to achieve if left to its own devices is thus depicted in heretical terms (Meadowcroft 2005). Those who bedeck themselves in heretical garb by asking for regulations that are cast through the prism of social rather than market justice are treated as sinners who know not what they do. However, the incredulity that there are still some people who do not see "the market" in the same light as the true believers is not enough on its own to ensure that the heretics will simply desist. The rhetoric of "the market", in other words, powerful as it might be in persuading atheists to see the world as agnostics do and agnostics as committed believers do, is never enough on its own to propel political outcomes. A whole host of institutional forms have consequently been brought to life over the last forty years and more to act as pro-market automatic pilots for policy (Rodrik 2007). The heretics are more easily quietened if their willingness to dissent is robbed of its avenues for political expression.

Every moment of new institutional architecture of this nature represents a point in time in which market institutions, the rhetoric of "the market" and the market concept become readily blurred. The institutions in question have to take on some sort of market form, otherwise they would be treated by the true believers as pandering unnecessarily to heretical counterclaims. The justification for moving to this new institutional reality is long on promise of the gains that will follow from removing potential political veto points from the management of the economy. Moreover, a body of economic theory has grown up over the same period as market ideology has regained its position of dominance that advocates strict adherence to the practical lessons that the market concept reveals (Obstfeld & Taylor 2004). The justification that this will always make macroeconomic policy more effective is a familiar refrain for anyone who has heard the political theologians speak. Even the name of the **policy ineffectiveness proposition** says volumes in this regard, suggesting that the government will always make matters worse if it tries to divert the economy from its ostensibly natural course (Sargent & Wallace 1975, 1976; Lucas 1976; Barro 1977; McCallum 1980). Viewed from this perspective, the alternative of simply letting "the market" find its own equilibrium will always put more money in people's pockets.

Again, think Mitterrand; think Thailand; think Bear Stearns. Think, in particular, about how many people were newly impoverished – lost their shirts even – as the status quo proved unsustainable due to adverse trading patterns on financial markets. Spot the difference here. From the perspective of the political theologians, they were subjected to entirely necessary correctional interventions because their avowedly anti-equilibrium activities meant that there were excessive welfare penalties to be paid unless a market equilibrium could be restored. The difference is between real impoverishment on the one hand and hypothetical welfare gains on the other.

It appears to be beguilingly easy to run together arguments about market institutions, the rhetoric of "the market" and the market concept, as it is far from clear where one sort of appeal stops and another starts. For instance, the practice of delegating policy-making responsibility to automatic pilots contained within market institutions does indeed seem to have a direct complement in the economic theory of policy delegation (Bénassy-Quéré *et al* 2010). The relevant theoretical tradition has its origins in the 1970s (Drazen 2000). This was a time at which the capitalist economy appeared to be incapable of being managed in a way that either protected jobs or protected the underlying price level (Blinder 1979). The previous Keynesian settlement, in which governments intervened in the economy to ensure that **aggregate demand** was kept high and inflationary pressures low, seemed to many observers to have been exhausted. In its place there developed a new form of political argument that said that government was the problem and that politicians had to be persuaded to find ways of restricting the reach of government into everyday economic life if the economy was ever to recover its former vibrancy (Gamble 2009). Given this context, it is not hard to see how the political rhetoric of "the market" might have begun to gain prominence. If government was no longer to be trusted to be the ultimate guarantor of economic stability, then "the market" could be presented as an alternative candidate to take its place. It is interesting to note in this regard that in neither its analytical nor its formalist phase does the market concept include any role for the government. It exists in an abstract space where it alone is the object of interest. It is therefore perhaps of no great surprise that economic theorists were able to devise policy-making models in which the mere presence of an actively-minded government is enough to lead to socially sub-optimal outcomes. These models have proved to be consistent with both a purist's account of the market concept (in the theorists' self-made abstract world) and the by now resurgent political rhetoric of "the market" (in the real world).

These policy-making models are all based on an assumption that policy-makers have to be "**credible**" if their stated policy goals are ever to be met (Forder 2000). However, credibility means something rather more specific in economic theory than it does normally. The believability criterion that is attached to the everyday meaning of the word remains central to its use in economic theory, but we do not have to dig very deeply to discover what else is implied. In ordinary language credibility revolves around whether it is reasonable to expect you to do what you say you are about to do, in recognition that the context in which you are seeking to act in a certain way simply might not be conducive to facilitating that action. In economic theory it is much more about whether anything you say should ever be considered trustworthy given your past history as a policy-maker. Policy-makers who are known to have intervened previously to secure short-term gains in social welfare will never be trusted to sit on their hands in future whatever they say about their subsequent desire to allow "the market" to take its natural course (Persson & Tabellini 1990). Finn Kydland and Edward Prescott both won the Nobel Memorial Prize in Economic Sciences for their original specification of the so-called **time consistency problem** (Kydland & Prescott 1977). Their basic argument was to beware later converts to the market faith, because the conversion might not prove to be real. Anyone who had a prior reputation for meddling in the affairs of "the market" by trying to engineer an increase in social welfare could not be trusted not to revert to type when tested in the future (Sargent 2013). Once a heretic always a heretic, this seemed to be saying.

The most important thing for current purposes is to understand what is going on in the background to these models. Consistent with the market concept in its analytical and formalist phases, every economic agent for the sake of the models' tractability is provided with full instrumental rationality. In this context everyone will choose to act in the way that benefits them personally the most in crudely self-interested terms. Moreover, in the time consistency tradition all economic agents are granted **rational expectations** (P.

117

Fisher 1992). That is, they inhabit a theoretical world in which they are able to know all future states, being aware of the heresies in which non-credible policy-makers will engage even before the policy-makers themselves become conscious of their next steps (Attfield, Demery & Duck 1985). They also know that the models have only one optimizing solution and that this is the equilibrium position in which "the market" will always ultimately settle if it is left to its own devices to freely come to that state (Sheffrin 1983). Walras's image of "the market" groping its way to its preferred solution is thus thrust back to the forefront of the discussion, but only if the end state of all that groping is predetermined by the model parameters with which the investigation began. Once again, the argument relies on treating "the market" as an "it" that knows its own desires. The conflation between the market concept and market ideology remains very close to the surface.

Time consistency problems are overcome within the theory by finding a way of tying the government's hands (Minford 1995). The early theoretical innovations in this regard focused on appointing policy-makers who already possess the reputational resources that would lead all economic agents to assume, even in the presence of rational expectations, that they would be true to their word (Barro & Gordon 1983; Backus & Driffill 1985). This might be seen as a variant of Walras's pledges model, in which the "*bons*" entered into by all economic agents ensured that they would be good for the commitments that they made about what to produce and when (see Chapter 5). In the time consistency tradition, though, it is policy-makers who have to be good for the commitments they make about not meddling with "the market". Kenneth Rogoff (1985) suggested that the government could emasculate itself most effectively by appointing a conservative central banker to make economic policy pledges on its behalf. Just as the word "credibility" has a special meaning in the time consistency tradition, so too does the word "conservative". A conservative policy-maker is one who finds it relatively untroubling to ignore society's demands for government intervention in the economy, because they do not share society's instinctive assumption about the shape of the social welfare function (Lohmann 1998).

This might, however, amount to nothing more than solution through conceptual sleight of hand. Policy-making in the Kydland-Prescott world reduces to a game between the private sector, which always by definition knows best what is right for the economy, and the government, which despite its good intentions equally by definition does not (Miller & Salmon 1985). Here, the private sector is constructed in a way that is identical to claims made on behalf of "the market". The government cannot steer the economy into a position of maximal efficiency because it shares society's preference for the more equal distribution of economic outcomes that real-life market institutions, in general, do not deliver. The conservative policy-makers to whom the government delegates authority to make policy decisions in Rogoff-type models is rather different (le Heron & Carre 2006). They are immune to internalizing society's distributional preferences because, in essence, they are not of society at all. This clinical detachment allows them to shadow the opinions of "the market" so closely that there is a formal conceptual identity between the conservative policy-maker and "the market". Both are perfect representations of the preferences of the private sector. With "the market" once again rendered as a thing in this construction, conservative policy-makers know what is best for the economy in exactly the same manner as "the market" does. Within the time consistency tradition at least, the conservative policy-maker is merely the human form of "the market" and therefore does all of its bidding for it.

The call for conservative policy-makers has never been more clamorous than within the context of the most recent period of economic globalization (Lavelle 2016). The global economy has become synonymous with the redrawing of the parameters of agential choice (Hassan & Kaynak 2013). Consumers, we are told, can now make use of online technologies to source for themselves the most competitively priced products from around the world. Producers, meanwhile, are alleged to have become essentially footloose, being able to locate their production wherever in the world competitive logic dictates. The optimizing plans of both consumers and producers have gone global, it seems. If this is true, though, then so too must the demand and supply curves of the classic demand-and-supply diagram. However, in a world in which consumers and producers have never had a more extensive range of choices than they do today, the most commonly told story is that this rebounds negatively on policy-makers so as to enforce a bland ideological conformity onto governments of all political stripes (Martell 2010). Economic globalization is widely assumed to have limited feasible macroeconomic policy to the one that credibility-based economic theory has argued for all along: namely, giving "the market" free rein to get exactly what it wants.

It seems to matter not that there must be various someones behind this particular image of "the market" and that it is they, and not "the market" itself, who are having their economic policy wishes fulfilled by conservative policy-makers. It also seems to matter not that the constitution for a global economy is being enshrined by international institutions to whom governments are willingly ceding so much of their macroeconomic autonomy. A single image dominates the public consciousness, that of an all-conquering market that has increasingly been able to project itself globally.

This sense that decentralized economic institutions are now materially pervasive has been greeted by their political proponents as evidence that the "end of history" has been reached. This phrase is most closely associated with Francis Fukuyama's (2006 [1992]) account, written in the context of the disintegration of previous Cold War realities, that western free market capitalism had emerged from the twentieth-century battle of political systems as the last economic alternative left standing (see also Hughes 2012). Nobody who has lived through the subsequent geopolitical upheavals of the last twenty-five years would ever mistake the "end of history" for a literal description of a seemingly ever more fragmented and ever more fractious world. Yet in one sense the claim does still seem to resonate. Part of the appeal of the Fukuyama thesis for those who were ready to believe it was that it seemed to capture the feeling that a new and indelibly global dimension had been added to economic relations and that, because of this, "the market" was now installed in its rightful place where it would remain unchallenged for evermore.

This version of events remains undimmed today, a quarter of a century after Fukuyama's pre-emptive proclamation of a new geopolitical era. Despite the very recent rise of a new populist nationalism in many western countries, and despite the continuing political appeal of religion in other regions, it takes very little to sound convincing when declaring that "the market" is now a global phenomenon. This has added significantly to the traction of market ideology. As Cox (2016) suggests, theologians have long wished for an eschatological moment in which they could announce that history has stopped and that the religious future would forever be modelled on the religious present. Political theologians of "the market" have discovered their own eschatological moment in the dawning of economic globalization.

THE RED HERRINGS OF "THE MARKET"

> "The trouble with a free market economy is that it requires so many policemen to make it work."
>
> Dean Acheson, US Secretary of State, 1949–1953

> "Those who believe that liberal democracy and the free market can be defended by the force of law and regulation alone, without an internalised sense of duty and morality, are tragically mistaken."
>
> Jonathan Sacks, Former Chief Rabbi of the United Hebrew Congregations of the Commonwealth

The question that remains is what lies behind the political rhetoric of "the market". We can safely rule out the possibility that this is just a literal description of the way in which real-life market institutions actually work. We know, then, that this is instead an image that the political theologians have constructed to win the argument for "more market, less government". The political rhetoric is distinct from the real world that it is used to gain control over. It is also distinct from the self-made abstract world in which economists investigate purely theoretical relationships. It is, by contrast, a normative façade that exists on top of a reality that is actually experienced very differently in everyday life to the way in which the rhetoric suggests it should be. What, then, are the characteristics of that reality? What does the seemingly constant repetition of the political rhetoric of "the market" serve to obscure? Are there parallel universes in operation here, one whose image is brought to mind whenever the virtues of "the market" are extolled, but another that is much more familiar from our day-to-day economic engagements?

Dean Baker (2010: 17) has recently argued that the whole "less-versus-more" perspective – should we have less "market", should we have more – is nothing other than one giant diversion. As such, it is routinely unhelpful if it is clarity of understanding that we are interested in, as opposed, say, to who has the most purple of prose. The less-versus-more perspective invites us to consider three interrelated questions. First, do we trust governments enough to feel comfortable with plans for welcoming more government into the economy? The time consistency tradition in economic theory sides with the policy ineffectiveness proposition in saying that the answer to this question should always be "no", but the relationships they model to come to this conclusion operate in a hypothetical realm in which it is possible to simply assume away all social problems. The question remains a live one beyond the parameters of this realm. Second, do we accept that the regulatory impulse should continue unchecked, even if this means being burdened by more rules in the future? "Remove red tape" is the consistent plea of those who believe that regulations protecting the interests of various economic stakeholders infringe upon their right to make money from the economy. There is no visual representation of market regulations, it should be noted, in the classic demand-and-supply diagram from which so many people derive their instinctive understanding of how markets work. Third, do we really want to wish ourselves into a social experiment in which pure market self-regulation becomes the order of the day? We should know by now that the clear-cut relationships of what Deirdre McCloskey (1994: 133) has called "blackboard economics" do not translate in any straightforward sense into real life. We really cannot ever hope to live within the pristine vectors that propel the mathematics through which solutions to the existence problem of general equilibrium can be obtained.

These three questions line up logically alongside one another, whereby the answer to any one of them will strongly condition what the most likely answer to the other two will be. Anyone who uses the political rhetoric of "the market" in a self-consciously pro-market manner is almost certainly going to argue "no", "no", "yes" respectively in response to the three questions. No other combination of answers would really make sense from their perspective. They will almost certainly think that they have good reasons to be suspicious of the prevailing degree of encroachment of the government into the economy, let alone be willing to entertain further encroachments. As adherents of "the market" and confirmed holders of the faith, they will be aware that they cannot believe at the same time in both the vibrancy and the dynamism of real-life market institutions and the benevolence of government interventions into the economy. These are simply incommensurable registers through which to think through the principles of economic justice. Within the former register it is a simple matter of faith that protective regulations incur economic costs and should therefore be scrapped. These sorts of costs can be modelled on the classic demand-and-supply diagram and they form the basis of deadweight-loss analysis pioneered by Jules Dupuit (1969 [1844]) and Fleeming Jenkin (2014 [1868], 2014 [1870], 2014 [1872]) in the middle of the nineteenth century (see Chapter 4). Viewed in this way, "the market" must always win out over all other economic systems. No wonder true believers usually apply a pejorative qualifying adjective in front of the word "capitalism" to describe the national economic systems in countries in which the political theologians of "the market" have made perhaps less headway than they have in their own countries. "Crony capitalism" perhaps remains the most evocative of these particular slights (Haber 2002; Kang 2002; Lewis 2013; Cave & Rowell 2015; Khatri & Ojha 2016; Pei 2016).

Baker's point, however, is that the logic running through these answers is at best dubious and, at worst, grossly misleading. It suggests that, on the less-versus-more spectrum, to endorse "the market" is synonymous with wanting to see fewer regulations that govern economic behaviour. More market, after all, is taken to be merely the other side of the coin to less government. And it is true that we often hear the political theologians of "the market" calling for a wholesale bonfire of protective controls. In this context, the political feel-good expression of the "free market" equates to being free from government regulations so that market logic can stand on its own in the search for the real-life equivalent of the equilibrium point in economic theory. It is also true that most politicians responded to economic globalization by saying that this created conditions in which the future bias must always be towards policies that promote deregulation. In the increasingly exacting competitive environment associated with globalization, we were told, only deregulated economies stood to prosper: the bigger the market (it was now global) the smaller the regulatory impulse should be (even being squeezed out of existence altogether in the extreme) (Steger 2017). Certainly, there have been many economists who have consistently made the argument since the 1990s that the optimal rate of taxation on capital in open economies is zero (Razin & Sadka 1991; Tanzi & Schuknecht 1997; Tanzi & Zee 1997). However, all of this was built on a false equation. The endorsement of more market does not imply *less* regulation at all, only a different *type* of regulation. The less-versus-more perspective forces into a quantitative framework what at heart is really a qualitative matter.

Other authors have previously also noted the tendency for the word "deregulation" to be taken too literally (Ménard & Ghertman 2009). It invokes the image of moving to a new policy setting in which some previously existing regulations have been sacrificed. Deregulation therefore appears to be about getting rid of what is already there, but what has actually tended to happen is that old regulations have been replaced by new ones. This change has been no less significant, however, because it has rewritten the whole character of what regulatory bodies are attempting to do as well as the whole content of what regulation is (Leys 2003). It means that the objectives of macroeconomic management are not the same as they once were and also, therefore, that the role of the government in enforcing those objectives is not what it was. More market in this regard equates to a brand new role for government within market institutions, not the creation of market institutions that have no role for government. For this reason, we see some scholars talk about the *re-regulation* of the economy under conditions associated with globalization, not its deregulation.

Steven Vogel (1996) has written about this in terms of the apparent tension between "freer markets and more rules". The tension here, though, is only from within the structure of the political rhetoric of "the market". If you think that that rhetoric accurately depicts existing conditions then you might be forgiven for expecting that the commitment to unleashing market forces will result in a systematic reduction in the number of regulations that govern market relations. But outside that one way of thinking there is every reason to expect that the number of regulations will stay at least the same. We need to go back all the way to the descriptive market concept to find economic theorists worrying about economic exchanges in which neither counterparty to the exchange takes advantage of the opportunity to inflict harm upon the other. However, just because it has long been unfashionable for economic theory to be conducted in these terms, this does not mean that economic regulators have become any less interested in this issue. Producers still have to be protected from unfair competition as their rivals seek to use subsidies and tax loopholes to artificially lower their costs. Workers still have to be protected from unscrupulous bosses who might otherwise try to get them to do things that are bad for their health, their well-being or their sense of dignity. Consumers still have to be protected from fraudulent selling activities so that they can be confident in what they are buying and the price at which they make their purchases.

Freeing "the market" does not remove the need for these regulatory protections. Indeed, if anything, it is likely to enhance that need. When presenting their market concepts in the analytical and formalist phases, economists may very well have assumed away the need for protective market regulations. They treat every economic agent identically: all are equally trustworthy, equally reputable and equally attentive to making money only in the most honourable manner possible. Most modern marketplaces, however, lack the face-to-face dynamics described in the image of the eighteenth-century marketplace, where if harm was to be consciously enacted on a counterparty it was necessary to be looking them in the eye as you did so. They are stretched over rather longer distances, they are much more impersonal and they might even entail no need to interact directly with another person at all (Murray & Overton 2015). The temptation to act in a potentially harmful manner is therefore an ever-present feature of modern marketplaces, and never more so than in the virtual marketplace in which an increasing amount of everyday economic activity takes place (Winn 2006; Riefa 2016). This is why the freer "the market" becomes the more it needs to be regulated.

Another way of looking at this is through Philip Cerny's (1997) notion of the "paradoxes of the **competition state**". Academics who were confronted by a qualitatively new phase of economic globalization in the 1990s and 2000s responded by asking how effective the state was likely to be if producers were increasingly untethered from national controls and could choose to locate wherever the cost incentives were most attractive (Rodrik 2012). A geographical mismatch was announced between a state that must remain locked in to its national territory and economic activity for which the whole world was now a feasible location. Majority opinion had it that the state would now only be able to do much less of what it had become used to doing, so much so in fact that the underlying welfare state form was under existential threat (Glatzer & Rueschemeyer 2005). Fuelled by ever more observations that state spending was being diverted to try to enhance the competitiveness of the national economy, it became common to hear academics declare the coming of the competition state. Politicians played up to this image by telling their publics to expect to see a state in retreat in the future (Watson & Hay 2003). However, identifying that the state was doing less of what it used to do is not at all the same as being able to show that the state was doing less per se.

The competition state was founded politically on the assumption that publics could be persuaded to ask for less so that resources could be diverted instead into investments in national competitiveness. What eventually transpired, though, was a situation in which the state provided for itself many more opportunities to transgress into people's lives in the name of that objective. The population itself was repositioned as an aid to the state's competitiveness objective, but to be so it had to accept that state officials were going to attempt to remake it anew. A competitive economy implies the need for an economically competitive population, but this entails it being disciplined into shape, which in turn is always likely to imply more rather than less regulation of everyday economic life. The paradoxes of the competition state are therefore quite simply explained. In Cerny's account at least, they arise from the fact that the political rhetoric focuses on freeing "the market", but that this is experienced in society at large as a decrease in the freedom to live your life the way you want in the absence of an ever more intrusive state telling you what you should and should not be doing in an attempt to assist the national economy in becoming more competitive.

The promise of a free market therefore does not stand up even in its own terms as a valid description of what results when market ideology is as dominant even as it is today. The proponents of the political rhetoric of "the market" often present their argument as if the freer market institutions become the more their divine characteristics are able to come to the surface, and the more their divine characteristics are able to come to the surface the more they are able to resemble in practice the dynamics that propel the process of economic adjustment in economists' market models. There is nothing but an abstract economic logic at play in those models, so why would we ever expect for actual markets to work in exactly the same way? This is where the controversy over the agential characteristics that are ascribed to all economic agents in the analytical and formalist market concepts once again becomes relevant. The only context in which actual marketplaces could be governed by the same internal dynamics as the market concept is if everybody is imbued with exactly the same dispositions to act as the abstract *homo economicus*, nobody is able to use inherited social advantages in an economically meaningful way, and there is no active conscience within society demanding compensation for those who lose out in such a world through no fault of their own.

In any other circumstances the more important issue is always likely to be what type of market regulations should there be rather than how many should be allowed to remain on the statute books. Despite all the claims on both sides of the political divide that freeing "the market" leads to having rather less politics within the economy, a very different conclusion is therefore more appropriate. It is that actual market institutions are always governed politically and that the choice of how to govern them will always ultimately be decided within the political arena. Using market institutions and ostensible "market sentiment" as an automatic pilot for economic policy might always appear to be evidence of the depoliticization of economic policy. Hearing politicians proclaim their limited ability to act contrary to market logic on society's behalf does, after all, remove many veto points from the democratic arena. Yet depoliticization is nothing other than an intensely political trend involving the replacement of one set of market regulations with another (Foster, Kerr & Byrne 2015).

CONCLUSION

"The American free market system is the greatest engine for prosperity and opportunity that the world has ever seen."

Ted Cruz, 2016 US presidential candidate

"Basically, the myth is that America has been founded on the free market; the government has done very little; it has thrived under trade. But actually, if you look at the history, this is actually the country that has succeeded most with protectionist policies."

Ha-Joon Chang, institutional economist,
University of Cambridge

There is no such thing, in practice, as the free market. The political rhetoric of "the market" plays very strongly to the idea that there is an unexploited potential in market institutions that can be released if only the government can be persuaded to do the principled thing and get out of the way. That potential has feel-good stories written all over it, because it is linked to wealth creation of hitherto undreamt of proportions and an economically just society in which everyone will receive their due rewards. "The market" – omnipotent, omniscient and omnipresent as it is – also manifests itself as a great leveller: in thingified form it ensures that nobody gets any less or any more than they deserve to get. Economists' market concept helps to create a parallel image for the self-made abstract world of which it can speak. Under marginal pricing theory, the last product in the market is sold for the precise price that the last consumer in the market is prepared to pay for it (Mandler 1999). Meanwhile, under marginal productivity theory, the last person to be employed in a particular production process receives the precise sum in wages that their labour contributes to that process (Pullen 2010). However, this pure economic logic at work in the hypothetical realm is not what we actually experience in the real world. There, the price at which exchanges take place is shaped not by something called the free market so much as by who gets to structure prevailing market regulations to their own advantage. The promises of the free market are therefore almost wholly fantastical.

Take the promise of wealth creation. At the rhetorical level the appeal to the entrepreneur as wealth creator remains extremely powerful. It can be quite discomforting to find yourself positioned politically antithetically to the people who seem to have it in their hands to enrich both you and the society to which you belong. In truth, though, the construction of the entrepreneur as wealth creator is merely a means of claiming a favoured vantage point from which to say that market regulations should be structured in the way that the business community wants and not in any other way (Essers *et al* 2017). It is a claim to political privilege and to have suspended other political actors' right to veto the incorporation of business interests into economic policy. It is not a description of what "the market" will bring to society if only it is left to its own devices. Even granting divine features to market institutions does nothing to change this. Actual wealth creation is a social process that also involves the state and its willingness to create the institutions out of which long-term economic innovation typically arises (Mazzucato 2015). Wealth creation is thus a collaborative exercise that revolves around the interaction between the decisions that were made by governments of the past, the decisions that are made by state officials in the present and the creativity of the workforce. It extends significantly beyond the actions of the fabled entrepreneur (Armstrong 2005; Williams & Nadin 2013).

Take also the promise of mutual enrichment across the whole of society. All market institutions in practice exist behind a legal edifice that is maintained via the activities of often very well-paid lawyers and accountants (Sikka & Willmott 2013). The entrepreneurial function is protected by the presence of a complex system of patent, copyright and intellectual property law. Intellectual property law is one of those aspects of the regulatory environment that has gone global through the creation of an international institution that is designed to act as a watchdog across all countries, the World Intellectual Property Organization (May 2007; Muzaka 2017). However, the body of law over which it presides creates a space in which the laws of "the market" act as a direct competitor. The latter would permit generic versions of patented goods to be supplied to the market at a fraction of the price of the patented goods, but the former expressly forbids it. It is well documented, for instance, that the profitability of pharmaceutical companies relies less on continued excellence in product innovation and more on the ability to use patent protection to hike prices (Shiva 2001; Chaudhuri 2005; Marcellin 2010; Azam 2016). Consumers, whether as individuals or public healthcare providers, are thus required to pay over-the-top prices. This is how most people experience the supposedly free market, not as a context through which the whole of society benefits but as a mechanism that can be captured by the interests of a few. Arguing to make it freer still only threatens to further widen the gap between promise and experience.

All of this, of course, has been known for some time. I really do not think that I am saying anything profoundly new here. The interesting point in this regard, then, is how a simple account of the very different reality that lies behind the promises of the free market has made no dint whatsoever in the political rhetoric of "the market". Indeed, it is difficult to imagine a time prior to today in which that rhetoric was ever more dominant than it is now. It is as if it has become fact resistant: the more it is shown to be a flight of fancy the more it seems to be uttered merely as a statement of common sense. Its use has become the only guaranteed entry point to political debate about the future of the economy. If you cannot speak the language of "the market", you tend to be treated as if you lack the authority to be allowed into that debate. Moreover, if you can speak the language of "the market" but choose not to do so, you tend to be accused of peddling a utopia that shows how detached you are from reality. The irony of this situation is that it is the political rhetoric of "the market" that appeals to a life that is not being lived in the present and that can also never be lived in the future. *It* represents the utopia in this discussion. It is market regulations that are ever present and not the divinity of the free market.

CHAPTER 7

CONCLUSION

WHAT I HAVE DONE

> "Generally speaking, we get the joke. We know that the free market is nonsense. We know that the whole point is to game the system, to beat the market or at least find someone who will pay you a lot of money, cos they're convinced that there is a free lunch."
>
> Ron Bloom, Senior official in the Obama administration

> "Capitalism should not be condemned, since we haven't had capitalism."
>
> Ron Paul, widely known as the intellectual godfather of the Tea Party Movement

There is almost certainly no way around the central conundrum running through this book. Economic theorists will certainly continue to build models based on their market concept, as this can plausibly be understood as their very raison d'être. Neither should we expect any sudden respite from hearing politicians talk about the future in ways that invoke this thing called "the market" that imposes its will on the whole economic environment. We might recently have witnessed the rise of a populist nationalism that is attempting to harness a backlash against globalization, but what is this in economic terms if not the flipside of market ideology? It is not the wholesale dethingification of "the market" that I have advocated, so much as an objection to the outcomes that its thingified presence has caused us to have to accommodate ourselves to. There is thus unlikely to be much change in the continued coexistence of the market concept and market ideology. But this will continue to present the problem of the single word "market" being used in two very different contexts and in two very different ways. Will we be able to trust ourselves in the future to always be able to distinguish the two uses from one another when all we hear is the one word? Given how difficult it ever is to call out a conflation of the two uses before the moment has passed, could we even trust ourselves to be able to do this just some of the time?

Hopefully the preceding chapters have helped in the task to separate the market concept from market ideology and to keep the historical development of three very different market concepts distinct from the ultimately confusing idea of "the market" as a discrete thing. However, I would surely be pushing it too far to suggest that the foregoing analysis can act as a fool-proof antidote to all potential misuses of the word "market". They are simply too numerous and too familiar from everyday life to fall prey to a single academic book and the effect that it might have on what will always be a limited readership. My aim has been much more modest. It has been merely to demonstrate how two incommensurable traditions of thinking about the one word "market" have grown up side by side. If it has also served to sound a caution regarding the pitfalls of conflating the two then that is all the better.

It is said so often that the language of "the market" is a language of economic theory then it has been an achievement in itself if the preceding chapters have given cause to no longer take such a claim for granted. I have actually gone further than this to argue that the implied line of causation is entirely fictitious. Economic theory has its market concept – indeed, it has at least three – but when economists give voice to market ideology then they are not speaking as economic theorists per se. They have jumped register to move from talking about relationships that are present only in their self-made abstract world of purely theoretical models to talking about relationships that they would like to see being brought to life in actual market institutions. Yet they do not require the authority that comes from being an economist to act politically in this way; the two processes are completely independent of one another. Some economists are willing to make such a move and to use the political rhetoric of "the market" to blur the distinction between their chosen market concept and market ideology. Their thingification of "the market" thus follows the classic pattern of saying not only that "the market" has the power to decide outcomes but also that this power should remain unimpeded because it leads to the best of all economic worlds. Other economists, by contrast, would never contemplate anything of this nature, because to do so is to try to imagine into being a type of world that politically they would not want to endorse. Given how frequently it is assumed that the language of "the market" is a language of economic theory, maybe it is necessary to point out just how many economists fall into this latter camp. It would be a considerable surprise if it proved to be anything other than a significant majority. After all, the marginalist techniques that have become synonymous with the demand-and-supply approach to economics were originally every bit as attractive to left-leaning economists as they were to right-leaning (Pilkington 2016). In sum, then, the thingification of "the market" clearly points in many different political directions at the same time, with the resulting diversity coming more obviously into view the more we look upon economists as a heterogeneous community.

Whichever side of the political divide economists associate themselves with is a matter solely of their own choosing and solely for their own conscience to pass judgement on. It is a matter of much broader concern that a great proportion of their number teach rudimentary knowledge of their subject field's underlying market concept in a completely ahistorical manner (e.g., Schabas 1992; Corry 2000; Kates 2013). Economics textbooks do not always do the present particularly well, as extensive treatment of the classic demand-and-supply diagram's account of partial equilibrium is usually accompanied by the merest of sketches of the idea of general equilibrium. The analytical market concept (what I have also described as the market concept in its Mk 2 phase) is thus allowed to almost completely drown out the formalist market concept (or the market concept in its Mk 3 phase). In many of the textbooks it stands alone and, through this process of omission, it becomes *the* market concept. If this is worrying enough, then the incomplete treatment of the past is even more marked than the incomplete treatment of the present. This goes beyond noting that most teaching texts in economics say nothing about the descriptive market concept that has its origins in the eighteenth-century study of actual marketplaces, as if the dominant meaning of a concept today can be understood outside the context of also understanding what it replaced. It is also that the dominant analytical market concept is presented in its settled form today absent of all the struggles over its initial development.

The great merit of taking a suitably historicized approach – as far as I see the matter in any case – is that it allows us to think more clearly about alternatives. The language that we hear most often much more readily implies agreement about a set way of both thinking about and doing things. Instead of being presented with the image of alternatives to choose between, we are much more likely to be confronted with the idea of *the* market concept (suggesting just one credible intellectual framework) and the idea of "*the* market" (suggesting just one accompanying economic logic). For anyone who has ever worried that this leads to either dull conformity of thinking or the political fatalism that there is now only one way of organizing society, relief is at hand in a suitably historicized approach. It helps us to understand how there has always been contestation over the best way of constructing a market concept that serves the purpose economists expect of it. Of course, that purpose is also a matter of contestation. A balance always has to be struck between a market concept that is, on the one hand, sufficiently abstract to allow clear-cut solutions to arise in economists' self-made model world and also, on the other hand, sufficiently realistic in its assumptions that it is possible to go at least some way to recognizing its real-world analogues.

It changes the perception of what economics is if it is no longer seen through the textbooks' lens of a homogenized body of work, but as a patchwork design of competing claims and counter-claims. The constant challenge involved in striking the above balance between abstract precision and real-life plausibility entails a never-ending struggle to define how best to produce for society at large a useable language of markets and marketplaces. The deceit of the textbooks is not so much that they want to show students what it means, in Mankiw's (2016: 19–46) words, to think like an economist, as that this tends to be constructed in singular terms. To think like an economist almost always means to alight upon the one way of thinking like an economist. A few deferential nods might be apparent to the existence of different schools of thought, but much more often than not these differences are presented against the backdrop of the same starting assumption of an identikit analytical market concept.

By attempting to restore some of the history to the market concept, then, it becomes increasingly possible to question what the textbooks typically tell us is a universal entity. The textbook representation is suggestive of what must have taken place to foster every exchange in every marketplace in all countries at all moments of time. This is a rendering that has pretensions to transcontextual application, which should immediately make us ask why the version of the market concept that features so prominently in the economics textbooks was developed only within the specific context of the mid-to-late nineteenth century. Should we really believe that the supposedly transcontextual phenomenon to which it relates was simply not spotted by anyone in the first four thousand years in which goods were being exchanged in marketplaces? All concepts have a history, and social science concepts in particular have a history that is linked to the specific circumstances in which they were first developed. This, though, is a matter on which the economics textbooks are silent when it comes to their central market concept, preferring instead to present it as a universal entity.

WHAT IS LEFT TO DO

"Marshall did something much more effective than changing the answer. He changed the question. For Ricardo the Theory of Value was a means of studying the distribution of total output between wages, rent and profit, each considered as a whole. This is a big question. Marshall turned the meaning of Value into a little question: Why does an egg cost more than a cup of tea? It may be a small question but it is a very difficult and complicated one. It takes a lot of time and algebra to work out the theory of it. So it kept all Marshall's pupils preoccupied for fifty years. They had no time to think about the big question, or even to remember that there was a big question, because they had to keep their noses right down to the grindstone, working out the theory of the price of a cup of tea."

Joan Robinson, "An Open Letter from a
Keynesian to a Marxist"

"The 'marginalist revolution in economics' is acclaimed by bourgeois economists as the theoretical revolution which freed political economy from extraneous political considerations."

Simon Clarke, *Marx, Marginalism and Modern Sociology*

It is always the case that more can be done. Even though economists, in general, may not always have shown the utmost interest in the history of their own subject field, this does not mean that everyone else should adopt a similar position. There is a popular view within economics that good theory will always drive out bad theory and that what is left standing will always, by definition, be the best possible theory. From this perspective, it might well be understandable that all the focus within the economics textbooks is on the market concept as it is generally understood today, not on the politico-historical conditions within which that concept originally arose, and certainly not on how the struggle to replace one variant of the concept with another occurred within these specific politico-historical conditions. Restoring the politics to the everyday language of "the market" might be matched by attempting to restore the politics to the intellectual context within which new directions were first entertained for the market concept.

There are only glimpses of a genuine discussion in the economics literature of how the relationships depicted in the classic demand-and-supply diagram relate to the broader politico-historical structures that were shaping all developments in thought at that time. It hardly needs to be said that the **Marginalist Revolution** in economics did not emerge from nowhere. It was part of the wider changes that were taking place within society in the mid-to-late nineteenth century (De Vroey 1975). A before and after comparison reveals a really rather momentous shift in both the object and the subject of economic theory. The object changed from a concern with understanding production as a social enterprise to understanding the characteristics of abstract moments of exchange (Clarke 1991). Whereas thingification of "the market" has become a familiar refrain in the latter period, it would have made no sense at all in the former. Prior to the Marginalist

Revolution, the very idea of the economy necessarily referenced the political context within which livelihood struggles took place, struggles over which of the social classes could best position themselves to lay claim to the surplus value that arose from the production process (Zweig 2005). Following it, the idea of the economy referenced instead the purely technical context within which the allocation of resources occurred, with economic theory becoming a means of adjudicating how efficient that allocation was (Sklanksy 2002; Trigilia 2002). The really big issue of social structure was therefore reduced to something significantly less grand (Meek 1974). In the process, the subject of economic theory changed from the all-round real-life social relations of production to individual, but always hypothetical, consumers and producers. As part of this change the space opened up for the ostensibly plausible thingification of "the market".

Modern-day defenders of the Marginalist Revolution typically depict it as the moment that economics first began to discover its true scientific mission (Keita 1992). Viewed from this perspective, it can only be a positive that economic theory became less reliant for its content on the temporary schisms of contemporary politics and instead was refocused on questions of underlying essence (Marchionatti & Cedrini 2017). If this is your position then it might well be understandable if you choose to start directly with the analytical market concept and act as though everything preceding it never really happened. However, there is also a counter-history of this shift to be found on the margins of the economics literature, and this concentrates instead on what was lost from the wider narrative regarding the economy when the focus moved away from the process through which surplus value was both produced and distributed (Düppe 2011). This counter-history emphasizes the egalitarian thrust of thinking in terms of surplus generation and asking who had the right to take surplus out of the economy. In many ways this was the central message of the descriptive market concept – do no harm unto others – but scaled up to the level of the whole economy. What replaced that particular variant of the market concept has none of the instinctive egalitarian presumptions of its predecessor.

Despite insisting that economists' market concept and the political rhetoric of "the market" must be treated as separate entities, then, it remains the case that there is a politico-historical backdrop to the development of each of the variants of the market concept. This backdrop is by no means determining of the content that eventually ensues, but it does help us to contextualize that content and to begin to comprehend why it emerged at the particular time it did. The descriptive market concept, for instance, arose against the backdrop of the development of the first commercial societies and as the world stood on the cusp of the Industrial Revolution (Muller 1993). Surely it is more than coincidence that as feudal ties were beginning to be relaxed economic theorists were asking whether the exchange relations that were replacing them would facilitate a functioning society within which people would happily consent to live (Reisman 2010 [1976]). Indeed, why would we expect them to have focused on anything other than this question? It was the biggest issue of their time and they are likely to have seen it as an abrogation of duty not to have tackled it.

Likewise, the development of the analytical market concept took place against the backdrop of political tensions over the living and working conditions that subsequent patterns of industrialization had wrought (Steedman 1995). The "do no harm" entreaties of the proponents of the descriptive market concept were clearly breached on a daily basis under conditions of nineteenth-century industrialization. If economic theory was to continue to comment on everyday affairs in this register, then it would clearly have pointed towards a brand new ownership structure that prevented a handful of owners from taking advantage of property laws to enact harm on countless others (Milonakis & Fine 2009). However, there was little appetite amongst the political elite for such a radical overhaul. The shift towards a more individualistic register for economic theory amidst the search for essential characteristics of market exchange thus proved convenient for the political status quo. The development of the formalist market concept also proceeded against a political backdrop that was heavily status quo oriented. The existence proof for the conditions of general equilibrium was presented in the context of the western world's Cold War struggle against communism (Bockman 2011). At this time there was a presumption towards political endorsement of "the market" in a distinctly thingified form, and the formalist market concept is often misread as a salute to the ability of market institutions to manage every aspect of social life both effectively and efficiently. In the hands of its pioneers, by contrast, the general equilibrium approach was much more likely to be used to illustrate the limits of trusting too much in the equilibrating dynamics of market institutions.

We could usefully learn much more about the way in which facilitative politico-historical circumstances have left their stamp on different variants of the market concept. For instance, the classic demand-and-supply diagram continues to be presented within the economics textbooks as if it unlocks the secrets to all economic issues and to so much more besides. Its ostensibly transcontextual nature is never questioned, because to do so would involve entering the territory of intellectual history, a territory that is generally considered to be somehow beyond the boundaries of economics properly understood. However, the analytical market concept was originally developed, it seems, as a means of avoiding having an economic theory that required the reader to imagine a world that was ripe for restructuring in a genuinely egalitarian direction. The strictly contextual has therefore been transformed through repeated use as a pedagogical tool into something supposedly transcontextual. But what does it mean for economics textbooks to have become so fixated on a single account of the market concept in this way? Are we required, if only by proxy, to continue fighting a mid-nineteenth-century argument that there is something essential in market processes that acts to withstand political pressures for greater equality within society? Is it not possible to devise our own market concept that better reflects how opinions about the world have moved on since that time?

"THE MARKET" AND DISTRIBUTIONAL POLITICS

"A businessman cannot force you to buy his product; if he makes a mistake, he suffers the consequences; if he fails, he takes the loss. A bureaucrat forces you to obey his decisions, whether you agree with him or not ... If he makes a mistake, you suffer the consequences; if he fails, he passes the loss on to you, in the form of heavier taxes."

Ayn Rand, libertarian novelist of *Atlas Shrugged*

"When I was poor and I complained about inequality they said I was bitter. Now I'm rich and I complain about inequality they say I'm a hypocrite. I'm starting to think they just don't want to talk about inequality."

Russell Brand, English comedian and political activist

This brings me closer to the conclusion of my discussion. I remain as adamant as ever about the necessity of treating the market concept and market ideology as distinct entities. They are linked too indelibly to discrete ontological realms to ever permit direct interchangeability. Where any single individual stands on the issue of market ideology is no clue in itself to what they will make of the market concept. The reverse is also true. Abstract economic conceptualizations and concrete political argumentation exist on different planes of thought and, as such, they are always going to be related in contingent, complex ways. That said, now that I have opened up the issue of the politico-historical conditions under which the various market concepts were first developed, it might be possible to posit a very different kind of relationship between the market concept and market ideology. If we know the politico-historical conditions in play when the various market concepts were initially committed to print, and if we can identify the live political issues of the day, we should then be able to ask whether the political rhetoric of "the market" today contains analogous features to the political arguments on display back then. None of this, to be sure, indicates that the market concept can be used on its own and in its own terms to make the relevant political argument, let alone to win it. But it would be indicative of a shared political mindset in which ideas about "the market" might be seen to resonate.

There is an important qualification to forward in this regard, which is whether the political mindset into which the various market concepts were projected did indeed allow for some such resonance. As suggested at the end of the previous section, it might be that in only one of the three cases studied in this book do we see any degree of alignment at all. The mid-to-late eighteenth-century market concept was founded on the image of broad social equality so that the moment of exchange did not advantage one counterparty over the other, even before either had expressed their willingness to transact. Actual market institutions of the time, though, were structured to enable deeply unequal practices of surplus extraction from the economy, with money undoubtedly being encouraged to follow money. Likewise with the mid twentieth-century concept of the market. It was founded on the image of social concerns about the extent to which market institutions failed to deliver outcomes that society would vote for and the frequency of the ensuing market failure. However, it was projected into a context in which politicians would go out of their way not to recognize the pervasiveness of market failure, for fear that this would be interpreted geopolitically as an admission of weakness. It was only the mid nineteenth-century market concept that seems to have been pitched into a permissive political mindset, as well as where we see clearly in evidence the potential for today's appeal to "the market" to reveal echoes of the politico-historical environment in which this particular market concept was first developed.

The dominant political mindset today is by no means conducive to allowing the restriction of property rights that was a notable part of the politico-historical environment out of which the market concept arose in its descriptive and formalist phases. Indeed, the most recent period of economic globalization has been embedded institutionally as much in the spatial extension of property rights as in anything else (Coleman 2011). The introduction of new spatial imagery into the thingification of "the market" cautions strongly against challenging such an outcome: "the global market", we are told, simply will not stand for anything else. International institutions have made their help for developing countries conditional upon demonstrating their respect for the rule of law, and this has had the effect of projecting property rights increasingly globally. This is consistent only with the politico-historical circumstances within which the analytical market concept was developed. If the counter-history of the Marginalist Revolution is correct and it is to be understood within the context of social struggles over who was to share in the surplus generated within the economy, we need to be thinking in terms of a future for property relations that was by no means assured. The thingification of "the market" has latterly created a commonly agreed political necessity out of what was never more than contestably contingent in its original form. Property was concentrated at that time in far fewer hands than is even true today, and as such it was relatively easy to show how harmful this was to the interests of a significant majority of people. The market concept that was developed in this period was not a simple expedient for winning the political argument against those who were insisting that the harms from the concentrated ownership of economic resources should be corrected. For one thing, abstract economic conceptualization and concrete political argumentation continued to exist in completely different analytical realms; for another, the political opinions of the marginalist pioneers are a matter of record and they were by no means status quo oriented on the so-called **Social Question** of the day (Paul 1979; Black 1982; White 1996). However, the gradual shift from the descriptive to the analytical market concept did take the discussion of property law out of economics (Beckert 2008).

This did not mean that economists in their totality suddenly stopped worrying about the structure of ownership within society. It was just that they could no longer address this issue from within economic theory and still lay claim to being mainstream theorists. Therefore they had to appeal to another source of authority beyond their professional reputations as economists when attempting to express such concerns. An ontological break thus occurred within economic theory that did nothing on its own to enforce a solution to the question of who should be allowed to own what, but it did provide indirect support of sorts for those who wanted to say that the state had no right to begin meddling in ownership by removing that issue from the realm of economic theory. Concentrating solely on the essence of abstract moments of exchange was a long way from arguing that ownership should be socialized so as to reduce the overall amount of harm on display within the economy.

It is by no means a stretch to suggest that very similar politico-historical conditions are instantly recognisable today. Perhaps one of the reasons why the analytical market concept features so prominently in economics textbooks of the most modern vintage is that it takes little to imagine the debate about property rights being transposed from the mid nineteenth century to contemporary times. The language in which the debate is conducted will have changed, of course, as will the philosophical principles on which the justification of private property is based. But if we were to look at the outline of the debate and focus on the political argument for why the state should think twice before socializing ownership, then nothing much is different. Those whose social or economic good fortune places a grossly disproportionate amount of property in their hands continue to be depicted as effective custodians of that property. It seems that they are to be trusted to maintain and invest in it in a way that would be beyond the capacity of a socialized ownership structure. For added rhetorical flourish it is often argued that it is "the market" that has allowed this concentration of ownership to happen, and in a context where it is readily assumed that "the market" always knows best then no more needs to be said, it would appear.

This still represents a jump from the market concept to market ideology, but it is a jump that nonetheless has consequences. The political rhetoric of "the market" is perhaps merely a front for arguments that enable redistribution to flow up income gradients rather than down them. It is more than coincidence that the **Occupy movement** has recently mobilized under the evocative banner of "We are the 99%". Research for Oxfam (2015, 2017) has shown the number of billionaires who own as much wealth as the combined total of the poorest half of the world's population to be falling sharply. This number was estimated to be 388 in 2010, 80 in 2014 and only eight in 2017. This is not so much the 1 per cent as the 0.000000001 per cent. 3.6 billion people (men, women and children) are being required to make do with as much as just these eight (all men) can call their own. They are not just the super rich, as they are much better described as the global super-duper-mega rich. They have amassed their eye-poppingly large fortunes behind a façade created by the political rhetoric of "the market", but in a reality in which market regulations have been systematically rewritten so as to favour their interests. Their property remains undiminished because their right to hold an unlimited amount has never been seriously questioned politically. When international institutions are required to construct a system of property rights that operates increasingly globally, this massive distortion of access to property is always the most likely outcome.

Equality is one of those concepts that it seems to be difficult to argue against. To say that you have a preference for equality over inequality appears to be the most reasonable position to take on the vast majority of issues. It gives the impression of confirming that you are interested in more than your own well-being and take seriously the claim that other people have also to see that their well-being is adequately attended to. Any other position would seem to make you insensitive to the lives that other people lead, uncaring even if the opportunities they have to flourish are significantly less advanced than your own. These are character traits, it should perhaps go without saying, that most people would be reluctant to attribute to themselves for fear that it would invite other people's immediate disapproval. And yet still inequality appears to have thrived recently in a way that is turning the clock back to the nineteenth century (Piketty 2014). It is more a feature of everyday life today pretty much throughout the world than it has been at any time in living memory. It is less critiqued, less challenged, less mobilized against. The ever more widespread use of the political rhetoric of "the market" as an all-seeing and all-knowing thing is one reason why.

That rhetoric is structured in ways that have a feel-good factor of their own to more than match the feel-good factor associated with the principle of equality. "The market" brings economic efficiency, we are told, and with economic efficiency comes new sources of wealth that everybody has the chance to share. In a classic case of blame the victim, when people complain that they have been turned into a source of wealth creation the benefits of which they are not invited to enjoy, a swift put-down tends to come their way. The political theologians will point out that their misfortune is down to their own inadequacies and not in any way to "the market". "The market", after all, treats everybody equally and also does the best for the whole of society. In this way, the responsibility for the spiralling inequality of outcomes is displaced into the realm of personal failings. "We are the 99%", the Occupy movement might well say, but in the way in which the political theologians recount the story of inequality the thing that separates the 99 per cent from the 1 per cent is aptitude. The latter has been blessed with what it takes to become rich, super rich or, in the extreme, super-duper-mega rich, whereas the former has not.

It is the regulations determining how market institutions function that ultimately make the difference between a more and less unequal experience of the economy. In situations like today where there is evidence of redistribution flowing up income gradients, this must mean that there is a permissive regulatory environment enabling such effects to occur. However, to govern in a context of increasing inequality necessarily has to remain a political choice. The political rhetoric of "the market" might well be used as a means of obscuring who has made that choice and through which channels it has been activated. The process of thingification erects a smokescreen around the assumption that the prevailing structure of distribution has been willed into being by an economic essence that is much bigger than any individual agent acting within the economy. However, someone somewhere must always have argued successfully for regulatory settings to be adjusted in such a way that greater inequality becomes the dominant direction of travel. Lots of other people must also have consented to the prospect that accelerating inequality will become the new reality. This is not an outcome that "the market" can ever generate on its own. And it is certainly not an outcome that can be attributed to the development of a particular variant of the market concept within economic theory.

FINAL WORDS

"The 'free market' is the product of laws and rules continuously emanating from legislatures, executive departments, and courts."

Robert Reich, former US Cabinet member

"Beginning in the 1970s, a wave of deliberate ideological, institutional and legal changes began to reconfigure the marketplace ... Inequality has been a choice."

Joseph Stiglitz, Nobel Laureate in Economics

It would be inappropriate to expect the economics textbooks to cover the same sort of territory as dominates the discussion in this book. They have their job to do, just as I have had mine. There is no reason to suppose that these two jobs should naturally align with one another. However, it still remains worthwhile whenever possible to step back from the content of the economics textbooks to pause and reflect. What is it that their authors think is the underlying purpose of their teaching texts? What is the task that they were designed to accomplish?

The most straightforward answer is to teach the basics of economic theory. However, it is a matter of some interest that these basics are reduced rather swiftly to students being required to learn two things. The first is how to manipulate abstract market relationships on the classic demand-and-supply diagram, the second is how to subject as many aspects of social life as possible to that one way of thinking. It was not always like this, though, because what is taken to be the foundation of economic theory today is far from the same as it has always been. Different types of economic theory have come in to and gone out of fashion in the past, and we should continue to expect multiple new challengers to emerge in the future. The fact that the analytical market concept has thus far managed to withstand all such challenges does not mean that it will do so for evermore. The classic demand-and-supply diagram provides us with just one view of what economics might be. Admittedly, most academic economists have a professional stake in it continuing to dominate. But it is nonetheless only one view amongst many of what economics should be, and there are glimpses of any number of alternatives already on show.

It is also a matter of interest how frequently we hear the argument that the market concept currently featuring so prominently in the economics textbooks is a vital constitutive part of contemporary market ideology. I have spent the whole of this book, however, making the counter-argument that the two should be understood to be distinct from one another, and it is much too late in the day now to start changing my mind. The two things are not the same at all, and neither are they related causally in any simple way. The most that the market concept and market ideology can share beyond the single word "market" is a common backdrop of being originally developed within the same politico-historical environment. This makes them no less independent entities of that environment, but it does at least provide us with a connection that might be explored further in the future.

And it appears to be a distinct possibility that plenty of time will present itself for these investigations to be undertaken. The analytical market concept and its accompanying visual representation in the classic demand-and-supply diagram do not look likely to loosen their grip anytime soon on the way in which the basics of economic theory are taught. In addition, the political rhetoric of "the market" looks set to be a pretty much ubiquitous feature of everyday life for some time to come. We are therefore likely to continue to be surrounded by both the market concept and market ideology, which suggests that the greater the sum of critical knowledge we can develop about both the better. It is to be hoped that this book at least makes a start on that endeavour.

GLOSSARY

aggregate demand: the level of demand within the whole economy, rather than just within a single market.

Alfred Tarski: a Polish American mathematical logician who spent the whole of his later career in the United States, having left Poland to undertake a speaking engagement in August 1939 and therefore being out of the country at the outbreak of the Second World War.

Chicago School: members of the Economics Department of the University of Chicago who are strong adherents both of the theoretical tradition of neoclassical economics and of the political doctrine of free market economics.

competition state: a state whose regulatory capacities are remodelled specifically to assist the country's international competitiveness.

consumers' surplus: the impression that some consumers experience additional utility due to the fact that they would have been prepared to pay more than the product's actual asking price.

continuous function: a mathematical function that passes smoothly through the gap between different units, rather than "jumping" from one unit to the next.

contract curve: the set of points resulting from two people trading their initial allocation of two goods under pure market conditions such that nobody can subsequently be made better off without the other person being made worse off.

Cowles Commission: more formally the Cowles Commission for Research in Economics, it was set up in 1932 using a donation from the US businessman Alfred Cowles; its scholars' major achievements have been in the fields of general equilibrium theory and econometrics.

credible: in macroeconomic theory a policy setting that the private sector can be reasonably sure the government will stick to.

deadweight loss: the amount of utility that cannot be recovered by the economy when a tax is in force.

demand-and-supply diagram: the classic two-dimensional representation of both sides of a market and its point of equilibrium.

demand-and-supply dynamics: buying and selling decisions typically taken to be the province of market institutions.

depoliticization: attempts to restrict the number of democratic veto points over the content of economic policy.

dethingification: reversing the previous process through which a conceptual abstraction has come to be treated as an actual thing, so that it has its identity as a conceptual abstraction unambiguously restored.

differential calculus: the aspect of the mathematical field of calculus that deals with the study of the rates at which quantities change.

equilibrium: defined in economics as the underlying state at which there is no tendency for change.

first best: in economic theory, this is the solution that arises when there are no constraints on reaching one objective caused by feedback effects from simultaneously reaching other objectives.

fixed-point theorem: the idea in mathematics that every continuous function must have at least one fixed point under certain conditions.

formalism: an approach to economics in which the precision of the mathematical form of the argument is considered to be more important than the realism of its economic content.

general equilibrium: a market model that seeks to show what a state of equilibrium looks like for all markets across all possible time periods.

hedonimeter: the machine suggested by Edgeworth that would compute exact levels of utility from signals emitted by the brain.

homo economicus: the abstract "economic man" who acts upon perfect knowledge of his behavioural environment to always conduct himself in the most instrumentally rational manner possible.

impartial spectator: Smith's concept referring to a conscience-like figure within the self that helps the individual to know whether their intended actions meet the standards of moral propriety.

indifference curves: curves conventionally drawn convex to the origin that depict the combinations of two goods that provide the consumer in question with an exactly equal level of satisfaction.

inelasticity: the feature of a product whose demand or supply is not particularly sensitive to price changes.

instrumental rationality: an approach to behaviour involving doing solely what is best for oneself.

Keynesianism: a type of macroeconomic policy named after John Maynard Keynes, through which governments intervene to keep both aggregate demand and social welfare high.

marginalist: an economist whose theories concentrate on what happens "on the margin", the last unit to be bought or sold.

Marginalist Revolution: the changing style of economic theory, typically dated to the 1870s, which eventually brought neoclassical economics to the fore.

market-clearing dynamics: the process through which demand perfectly matches supply and there are neither too many nor too few goods in circulation.

market coordination: the appearance that countless acts of decentralized economic decision-making follow a coherent pattern, as if through direct coordination.

market coordination problem: how to explain as an economic matter the way in which market-clearing dynamics operate across different markets to leave the whole of the market system in equilibrium.

mutual funds: a collective investment vehicle where an individual pays in but leaves all decisions regarding portfolio composition to the fund's investment managers.

mutual sympathy: a position in Smith's moral theory where the impartial spectators of two people are in perfect harmony with one another, instructing both to come to the same moral judgement about the contributions of each to the event in question.

neoclassical economics: an abstract body of economic theory that locates the essence of all rational economic behaviour in demand-and-supply dynamics.

neoliberalism: an approach to macroeconomic policy consistent with state retreat and the privileging of business interests.

Nicolas Bourbaki: a collective of French formalist mathematicians who wrote under a pseudonym named after a former army general, specializing in attempts to provide the rigorous underpinnings of a self-contained set theory.

Occupy movement: the global grassroots organization formed after the global financial crisis to protest against accelerating inequality.

oligopoly: a market structure dominated by very few producers, all of whom therefore exercise significant influence over both consumer choice and market price.

on the margin: a phrase in economics that refers to the last unit, whether this is the last unit consumed (consumption on the margin), the last unit produced (production on the margin), etc.

partial equilibrium: a market model that seeks to show what a state of equilibrium looks like for a market in one good at one moment in time.

pegged exchange rate regime: what results when the government decides to fix the value of its country's currency against the value of another country's currency or, more likely, against the value of a basket of other currencies.

pledges model: the final version of Walras's general equilibrium model, in which all consumers and producers are required to lock in their economic activities by pledging before-the-fact how they will act in every imaginable set of future circumstances.

policy ineffectiveness proposition: a body of macroeconomic theory from the 1970s stating that, no matter what sort of policies it introduces, government intervention can never raise the trend rate of growth of the economy.

price discrimination: the strategy of charging a different price for identical units of the same good, depending on what each individual consumer is willing to pay.

process theology: a view of the deity that insists its capacities are still in the making and not yet fully developed.

producers' surplus: the impression that some producers make greater-than-normal profits because they could have still supplied the market with their product at a lower asking price.

public goods: goods from which everyone benefits but no single person has a commercial incentive to produce on their own, therefore normally provided by the state out of the receipts from general taxation.

rational expectations: expectations that are generated when economic agents are deemed to know all future states of the economy.

regulatory arbitrage: attempts to play off one country's policy-makers against another's so as to gain commercial advantage.

representative individual: the instrumentally-rational person whose decisions stand in for the operation of perfect market-clearing dynamics.

revealed preference: the assumption that instrumental rationality can be read off from the observation of behaviour: the option chosen must necessarily have maximized utility for it to have been chosen in the first place.

second best: in economic theory, the most favourable solution that can be reached when accepting that there are constraints within the system that make the first best unattainable.

Social Question: the realization towards the end of the nineteenth century that rapid economic advances associated with industrialization brought with them more intense experiences of social dislocation.

sympathy: in Smith's moral theory, the act of generating fellow-feeling with others.

tâtonnement: the economic process described by Walras through which a market "gropes" its way towards equilibrium on the back of repeated buying and selling decisions.

thingification: the attempt to treat a conceptual abstraction as if it was an actual thing,

three-body problem: a mathematical problem regarding relative motions of more than two bodies, showing the limits of differential calculus.

time consistency problem: policy-making dilemmas arising when the private sector believes that the government has no incentive to abide by its pre-announced policy course.

transfer pricing: the nominal price that a company charges itself to "sell" the latest stage of a product's route to completion to its own operations in another country.

turning points: in mathematics, a maximum or minimum point on a curve.

utility: the economic measure of the enjoyment that follows from consuming a particular product.

BIBLIOGRAPHY

Ackerman, F. & A. Nadal 2004. "Introduction: Underneath the Flawed Foundations". In F. Ackerman & A. Nadal with C. Benetti, K. Gallagher & C. Salas, *The Flawed Foundations of General Equilibrium: Critical Essays on Economic Theory*, pp. 1–13. London: Routledge.

Alexander, P. 2015. *Corporate Social Irresponsibility*. London: Routledge.

Amadae, S. M. 2003. *Rationalizing Capitalist Democracy: The Cold War Origins of Rational Choice Liberalism*. Chicago, IL: University of Chicago Press.

Armstrong, P. 2005. *Critique of Entrepreneurship: People and Policy*. Basingstoke: Palgrave Macmillan.

Arrow, K. 1973. "Social responsibility and economic efficiency". Reprinted in *Collected Papers of Kenneth J. Arrow, Vol. 6: Applied Economics*, pp. 130–42. Cambridge, MA: Harvard University Press, 1985.

Arrow, K. 1983. "A difficulty in the concept of social welfare". In *Collected Papers of Kenneth J. Arrow, Vol. 1: Social Choice and Justice*, pp. 1–29. Cambridge, MA: Harvard University Press, 1983.

Arrow, K. 1987. "Oral history I: an interview". In G. Feiwel (ed.) *Arrow and the Ascent of Modern Economic Theory*, pp. 191–242. London: Macmillan.

Arrow, K. & G. Debreu 1954. "Existence of an equilibrium for a competitive economy", *Econometrica* 22:3, pp. 265–90.

Arrow, K. & F. Hahn 1971. *General Competitive Analysis*. San Francisco, CA: Holden Day.

Aspromourgos, T. 1996. *On the Origins of Classical Economics: Distribution and Value from William Petty to Adam Smith*. London: Routledge.

Attfield, C., D. Demery & N. Duck 1985. *Rational Expectations in Macroeconomics: An Introduction to Theory and Evidence*. Oxford: Blackwell.

Aumann, R. 1964. "Markets with a continuum of traders", *Econometrica* 32:1/2, pp. 39–50.

Aydinonat, E. 2008. *The Invisible Hand in Economics: How Economists Explain Unintended Social Consequences*. London: Routledge.

Azam, M. 2016. *Intellectual Property and Public Health in the Developing World*. Cambridge: Open Book Publishers.

Backhouse, R. 2002. *The Penguin History of Economics*. London: Penguin.

Backus, D. & J. Driffill 1985. "Inflation and reputation", *American Economic Review* 75:3, pp. 530–38.

Baker, A. 2014. "Transnational technocracy and the macroprudential paradox". In T. Porter (ed.), *Transnational Financial Regulation after the Crisis*, pp. 29–49. London: Routledge.

Baker, D. 2010. *Taking Economics Seriously*. Cambridge, MA: MIT Press.

Bamber, B. & A. Spencer 2008. *Bear Trap: The Fall of Bear Stearns and the Panic of 2008*. New York: Brick Tower Press.

Barro, R. 1977. "Unanticipated money growth and unemployment in the United States", *American Economic Review* 67:2, pp. 101–15.

Barro, R. 2008. *Macroeconomics: A Modern Approach*. Mason, OH: Thomson.

Barro, R. & D. Gordon 1983. "Rules, discretion and reputation in a model of monetary policy", *Journal of Monetary Economics* 12:1, pp. 101–21.

Barrow-Green, J. 1997. *Poincaré and the Three-Body Problem*. New York: American Mathematical Society.

Bayman, H. 2001. "Nietzsche, God, and Doomsday: The Consequences of Atheism". In W. Santaniello (ed.) *Nietzsche and the Gods*, pp. 183–212. Albany, NY: SUNY Press.

Beaud, M. & G. Dostaler 1997. *Economic Thought Since Keynes: A History and Dictionary of Major Economists*, trans. V. Cauchemez with E. Litwack. London: Routledge.

Beckert, J. 2008. *Inherited Wealth*, trans. T. Dunlap. Princeton, NJ: Princeton University Press.

Beckstein, M. 2016. *The Politics of Economic Life*. London: Routledge.

Begg, D., S. Fischer & R. Dornbusch 2008. *Economics*, ninth edition. New York: McGraw-Hill.

Bénassy-Quéré, A., B. Cœuré, P. Jacquet & J. Pisani-Ferry 2010. *Economic Policy: Theory and Practice*. Oxford: Oxford University Press.

Benetti, C., A. Nadal & C. Salas 2004. "The Law of Supply and Demand in the Proof of Existence of General Competitive Equilibrium". In F. Ackerman & A. Nadal with C. Benetti, K. Gallagher & C. Salas, *The Flawed Foundations of General Equilibrium: Critical Essays on Economic Theory*, pp. 68–85. London: Routledge.

Bernstein, M. 2003. "American economists and the 'marginalist revolution': notes on the intellectual and social contexts of professionalization", *Journal of Historical Sociology* 16:1, pp. 135–80.

Black, R. D. C. 1982. "The Papers and Correspondence of William Stanley Jevons: A Supplementary Note", *The Manchester School* 50:4, pp. 417–28.

Blaug, M. 1996. *Economic Theory in Retrospect*, fifth edition. Cambridge: Cambridge University Press.

Blinder, A. 1979. *Economic Policy and the Great Stagflation*. New York: Academic Press.

Block, D. 2012. "Georges Lemaître and Stigler's Law of Eponymy". In R. Holder & S. Mitton (eds), *Georges Lemaître: Life, Science and Legacy*, pp. 89–96. New York: Springer.

Block, F. & M. Somers 2014. *The Power of Market Fundamentalism: Karl Polanyi's Critique*. Cambridge, MA: Harvard University Press.

Blyth, M. 2002. *Great Transformations: Economic Ideas and Institutional Change in the Twentieth Century*. Cambridge: Cambridge University Press.

Bockman, J. 2011. *Markets in the Name of Socialism: The Left-Wing Origins of Neoliberalism*. Stanford, CA: Stanford University Press.

Boulding, K. 1971. "After Samuelson, who needs Adam Smith?", *History of Political Economy* 3:2, pp. 225–37.

Bowley, A. 1924. *The Mathematical Groundwork of Economics*. Oxford: Clarendon Press.

Bridel, P. 2011. "The Normative Origins of General Equilibrium Theory; or Walras's Attempts at Reconciling Economic Efficiency with Social Justice". In P. Bridel (ed.) *General Equilibrium Analysis: A Century After Walras*, pp. 15–23. London: Routledge.

Brooks, R. 2013. *The Great Tax Robbery: How Britain Became a Tax Haven for Fat Cats and Big Business*. London: Oneworld.

Brouwer, L. 1911. "Beweis der invarianz der dimensionenzahl", *Mathematische Annalen* 70:2, pp. 161–5.

Brown, V. 1994. *Adam Smith's Discourse: Canonicity, Commerce and Conscience*. London: Routledge.

Brown, W. 2015. *Undoing the Demos: Neoliberalism's Stealth Revolution*. New York: Zone.

Brownlie, A. D. & M. F. Lloyd Pritchard 1963. "Professor Fleeming Jenkin, 1833–1885: pioneer in engineering and political economy", *Oxford Economic Papers* 15:3, pp. 204–16.

Bulhof, I. & L. ten Kate 2000. "Echoes of an Embarrassment: Philosophical Perspectives on Negative Theology – An Introduction". In I. Bulhof & L. ten Kate (eds), *Flight of the Gods: Philosophical Perspectives on Negative Theology*, pp. 1–57. New York: Fordham University Press.

Burnham, P. 2001. "New Labour and the politics of depoliticization", *British Journal of Politics and International Relations* 3:2, pp. 127–49.

Callaghan, J. 2000. *The Retreat of Social Democracy*. Manchester: Manchester University Press.

Campbell, R. H. & A. Skinner 1976. "General Introduction", in A. Smith (1981 [1776/1784]) *An Inquiry into the Nature and Causes of the Wealth of Nations*, pp. 1–60. Indianapolis, IN: Liberty Fund.

Cave, T. & A. Rowell 2015. *A Quiet Word: Lobbying, Crony Capitalism and Broken Politics in Britain*. London: Vintage.

Cerny, P. 1997. "Paradoxes of the competition state: the dynamics of political globalization", *Government and Opposition* 32:2, pp. 251–74.

Chaudhuri, S. 2005. *The WTO and India's Pharmaceuticals Industry: Patent Protection, TRIPS, and Developing Countries*. Oxford: Oxford University Press.

Chipman, J. 2014. *German Utility Theory: Analysis and Translations*. London: Routledge.

Christ, C. 1994. "The Cowles Commission's contributions to econometrics at Chicago, 1939–1955", *Journal of Economic Literature* 32:1, pp. 30–59.

Clarke, S. 1991. *Marx, Marginalism and Modern Sociology: From Adam Smith to Max Weber*, second edition. London: Macmillan.

Clouder, S. & R. Harrison 2005. "The Effectiveness of Ethical Consumer Behaviour". In R. Harrison, T. Newholm & D. Shaw (eds), *The Ethical Consumer*, pp. 89–104. London: Sage.

Clower, R. 1995. "Axiomatics in economics", *Southern Economic Journal* 62:2, pp. 307–19.

Cobb, J. 2016. *Process Theology as Political Theology.* Eugene, OR: Wipf & Stock.

Cohan, W. 2009. *House of Cards: How Wall Street's Gamblers Broke Capitalism.* London: Allen Lane.

Cohen, G. A. 1995. *Self-Ownership, Freedom and Equality.* Cambridge: Cambridge University Press.

Colander, D. 2007. "Edgeworth's hedonimeter and the quest to measure utility", *Journal of Economic Perspectives* 21:2, pp. 215–25.

Cole, A. 1994. *François Mitterrand: A Study in Political Leadership.* London: Routledge.

Coleman, W. (ed.) 2011. *Property, Territory, Globalization: Struggles Over Autonomy.* Toronto: UBC Press.

Collard, D. 1973. "Léon Walras and the Cambridge caricature", *Economic Journal* 83:2, pp. 465–76.

Cook, S. 2009. *The Intellectual Foundations of Alfred Marshall's Economic Science: A Rounded Globe of Knowledge.* Cambridge: Cambridge University Press.

Corrick, L. 2016. "The Taxation of Multinational Enterprises". In T. Pogge & K. Mehta (eds), *Global Tax Fairness*, pp. 173–203. Oxford: Oxford University Press.

Corry, B. 2000. "Reflections on the History of Economic Thought or 'A Trip Down Memory Lane'". In A. Murphy & R. Prendergast (eds), *Contributions to the History of Economic Thought: Essays in Honour of R. D. C. Black*, pp. 55–69. London: Routledge.

Cournot, A. A. 1897 [1838]. *Researches into the Mathematical Principles of the Theory of Wealth*, trans. N. Bacon. London: Macmillan.

Cox, H. 2016. *The Market as God.* Cambridge, MA: Harvard University Press.

Craft, J. & M. Howlett 2017. "Trends Towards the Externalization of Policy Advice in Policy Formulation". In M. Howlett & I. Mukherjee (eds), *Handbook of Policy Formulation*, pp. 491–503. Cheltenham: Elgar.

Crouch, C. 2011. *The Strange Non-Death of Neoliberalism.* Cambridge: Polity.

Currie, M. & I. Steedman 1990. *Wrestling with Time: Problems in Economic Theory.* Cambridge: Cambridge University Press.

D'Amico, S. 2012. *Spanish Milan: A City within the Empire, 1535–1706.* Basingstoke: Palgrave Macmillan.

Daugberg, C. & A. Swinbank 2009. *Ideas, Institutions, and Trade: The WTO and the Curious Role of EU Farm Policy in Trade Liberalization.* Oxford: Oxford University Press.

Davidoff, S. 2009. *Gods at War: Shotgun Takeovers, Government by Deal, and the Private Equity Implosion.* New York: Wiley.

De Vroey, M. 1975. "The transition from classical to neoclassical economics: a scientific revolution", *Journal of Economic Issues* 9:3, pp. 415–39.

Debreu, G. 1984. "Economic theory in the mathematical mode", *American Economic Review* 74:3, pp. 267–78.

Debreu, G. 1986. "Theoretic models: mathematical form and economic content", *Econometrica* 54:6, pp. 1259–70.

Debreu, G. 1987. "Oral history II: an interview". In G. Feiwel (ed.), *Arrow and the Ascent of Modern Economic Theory*, pp. 243–57. London: Macmillan.

Debreu, G. 1991. "The mathematization of economic theory", *American Economic Review* 81:1, pp. 1–7.

DeCanio, S. 2014. *Limits of Economic and Social Knowledge*. Basingstoke: Palgrave Macmillan.

Dorfman, J. 1941. "The Seligman Correspondence III", *Political Science Quarterly* 56:3, pp. 392–419.

Dow, S. 2016. "Codes of Ethics for Economists, Pluralism, and the Nature of Economic Knowledge". In G. DeMartino & D. McCloskey (eds), *The Oxford Handbook of Professional Economic Ethics*, pp. 750–64. Oxford: Oxford University Press.

Dowd, K. & M. Hutchinson 2010. *Alchemists of Loss: How Modern Finance and Government Intervention Crashed the Financial System*. New York: Wiley.

Drazen, A. 2000. *Political Economy in Macroeconomics*. Princeton, NJ: Princeton University Press.

Düppe, T. 2011. *The Making of the Economy: A Phenomenology of Economic Science*. Lanham, MD: Lexington.

Düppe, T. 2012a. "Gerard Debreu's secrecy: his life in order and silence", *History of Political Economy* 44:3, pp. 413–49.

Düppe, T. 2012b. "Arrow and Debreu de-homogenized", *Journal of the History of Economic Thought* 34:4, pp. 491–514.

Düppe, T. & R. Weintraub 2014. *Finding Equilibrium: Arrow, Debreu, McKenzie and the Problem of Scientific Credit*. Princeton, NJ: Princeton University Press.

Dupuit, J. 1969 [1844]. "On the Measurement of the Utility of Public Works". In K. Arrow & T. Scitovsky (eds), *Readings in Welfare Economics*, pp. 255–83. London: Allen & Unwin, 1969.

Dyson, K. & K. Featherstone 1998. "EMU and Presidential Leadership under François Mitterrand". In M. Maclean (ed.), *The Mitterrand Years: Legacy and Evaluation*, pp. 89–111. Basingstoke: Palgrave Macmillan.

Eagleton-Pierce, M. 2016. *Neoliberalism: The Key Concepts*. London: Routledge.

Edgeworth, F. Y. 2003 [1881]. *Mathematical Psychics and Further Papers on Political Economy*, P. Newman (ed.). Oxford: Oxford University Press.

Ekelund, R. & R. Hébert 2014. *A History of Economic Theory and Method*, sixth edition. Long Grove, IL: Waveland Press.

Erickson, P. 2015. *The World the Game Theorists Made*. Chicago, IL: University of Chicago Press.

Essers, C., P. Dey, D. Tedmanson & K. Verduyn 2017. "Critical Entrepreneurship Studies: A Manifesto". In C. Essers, P. Dey, D. Tedmanson & K. Verduyn (eds), *Critical Perspectives on Entrepreneurship: Challenging Dominant Discourses*, pp. 1–14. London: Routledge.

Evensky, J. 2005. *Adam Smith's Moral Philosophy: A Historical and Contemporary Perspective on Markets, Law, Ethics, and Culture*. Cambridge: Cambridge University Press.

Fairtrade International 2017. *Monitoring the Scope and Benefits of Fair Trade*, eighth edition. Bonn: Fairtrade International.

Farley, W. 1990. *Tragic Vision and Divine Compassion: A Contemporary Theodicy.* Louisville, KY: John Knox Press.

Farlow, A. 2013. *Crash and Beyond: Causes and Consequences of the Global Financial Crisis.* Oxford: Oxford University Press.

Fine, B. 2004. "Economics Imperialism as Kuhnian Revolution?" In P. Arestis & M. Sawyer (eds), *The Rise of the Market: Critical Essays on the Political Economy of Neo-liberalism*, pp. 107–44. Cheltenham: Elgar.

Fiori, S. 2001. "Visible and invisible order: the theoretical duality of Smith's political economy", *European Journal of the History of Economic Thought* 8:4, pp. 429–48.

Fisher, F. 1987. "Adjustment Process and Stability". In J. Eatwell, M. Milgate & P. Newman (eds), *The New Palgrave: A Dictionary of Economics*, Vol. 1, pp. 26–29. London: Macmillan.

Fisher, F. 2003. "Disequilibrium and Stability". In F. Petri & F. Hahn (eds), *General Equilibrium: Problems and Prospects*, pp. 78–94. London: Routledge.

Fisher, P. 1992. *Rational Expectations in Macroeconomic Models.* New York: Springer.

Fitzgibbons, A. 1995. *Adam Smith's System of Liberty, Wealth, and Virtue: The Moral and Political Foundations of* The Wealth of Nations. Oxford: Clarendon Press.

Fleischacker, S. 2004. *On Adam Smith's* Wealth of Nations. Princeton, NJ: Princeton University Press.

Flinders, M. & J. Buller 2006. "Depoliticization: principles, tactics and tools", *British Politics* 1:3, pp. 293–318.

Force, P. 2003. *Self-Interest before Adam Smith: A Genealogy of Economic Science.* Cambridge: Cambridge University Press.

Forder, J. 2000. "The theory of credibility: confusions, limitations and dangers", *International Papers in Political Economy* 7:2, pp. 1–40.

Forman-Barzilai, F. 2005. "Sympathy in space(s): Adam Smith on proximity", *Political Theory* 33:2, pp. 189–217.

Foster, E. A., P. Kerr & C. Byrne 2015. "Rolling Back to Roll Forward: Depoliticization and the Extension of Government". In M. Flinders & M. Wood (eds), *Tracing the Political: Depoliticization, Governance and the State*, pp. 117–38. Bristol: Policy Press.

Fukuyama, F. 2006 [1992]. *The End of History and the Last Man.* New York: Free Press.

Galbraith, J. 2002. "The importance of being sufficiently equal", *Social Philosophy and Policy* 19:1, pp. 201–24.

Gamble, A. 2009. *The Spectre at the Feast: Capitalist Crisis and the Politics of Recession.* Basingstoke: Palgrave Macmillan.

Geanakoplos, J. 2004. "The Arrow-Debreu model of general equilibrium", *Cowles Foundation Paper*, No. 1090, New Haven, CT: Yale University.

Gereffi, G. 2014. "Risks and opportunities of participation in global value chains", World Bank Policy Research Working Papers, No. 6847.

Giggie, J. & D. Winston 2002. "Hidden in Plain Sight: Religion and Urban Commercial Culture in Modern North America". In J. Giggie & D. Weston (eds), *Faith in the*

Market: Religion and the Rise of Urban Commercial Culture, pp. 1–10. New Brunswick, NJ: Rutgers University Press.

Ginzberg, E. 2002. *Adam Smith and the Founding of Market Economics*, new edition. New Brunswick, NJ: Transaction.

Glatzer, M. & D. Rueschemeyer 2005. *Globalization and the Future of the Welfare State*. Pittsburgh, PA: University of Pittsburgh Press.

Grabel, I. 2003. "Averting crisis? Assessing measures to manage financial integration in emerging economies", *Cambridge Journal of Economics* 27:3, pp. 317–36.

Greenberg, A. 2010. *The Rise and Fall of Bear Stearns*. New York: Simon & Schuster.

Griffith-Jones, S. with J. Cailloux & S. Pfaffenzeller 1998. "The East Asian financial crisis: a reflection on its causes, consequences and policy implications", Institute of Development Studies Discussion Paper, No. 367.

Grimmer-Solem, E. 2003. *The Rise of Historical Economics and Social Reform in Germany 1864–1894*. Oxford: Oxford University Press.

Griswold, C. 1999. *Adam Smith and the Virtues of Enlightenment*. Cambridge: Cambridge University Press.

Groenewegen, P. 1973. "A note on the origin of the phrase, 'supply and demand'", *Economic Journal* 83:2, pp. 505–09.

Guesnerie, R. 2011. "On the Modernity of Walras". In P. Bridel (ed.), *General Equilibrium Analysis: A Century After Walras*, pp. 134–44. London: Routledge.

Gupta, R. K. 2017. *Recent Trends in Transfer Pricing: Intangibles, GAAR and BEPS*. London: Bloomsbury.

Haber, S. (ed.) 2002. *Crony Capitalism and Economic Growth in Latin America: Theory and Evidence*. Stanford, CA: Hoover Institution Press.

Hahn, F. 1973a. *On the Notion of Equilibrium in Economics*. Cambridge: Cambridge University Press.

Hahn, F. 1973b. "The Winter of Our Discontent", *Economica* 40:3, pp. 322–30.

Hall, P. (ed.) 1989. *The Political Power of Economic Ideas: Keynesianism Across Nations*. Princeton, NJ: Princeton University Press.

Hart, N. 2012. *Equilibrium and Evolution: Alfred Marshall and the Marshallians*. Basingstoke: Palgrave Macmillan.

Harvey, D. 2005. *A Brief History of Neoliberalism*. Oxford: Oxford University Press.

Hassan, S. & E. Kaynak (eds) 2013. *Globalization of Consumer Markets: Structures and Strategies*. London: Routledge.

Hay, C. & D. Wincott 2012. *The Future of European Welfare Capitalism*. Basingstoke: Palgrave Macmillan.

Heilbroner, R. 1986. *The Essential Adam Smith*. New York: Norton.

Hennings, K. 1979. "Karl Heinrich Rau and the graphic representation of supply and demand", Diskussionspapiere des Fachbereichs Wirtschaftswissenschaften der Universität Hannover, C35, Hannover: University of Hannover.

Hindmoor, A. 2017. *What's Left Now? The History and Future of Social Democracy*. Oxford: Oxford University Press.

Hirsch, M. & S. Smale 1974. *Differential Equations, Dynamical Systems, and Linear Algebra*. New York: Academic Press.

Hodgson, G. 2001. *How Economics Forgot History: The Problem of Historical Specificity in Social Science*. London: Routledge.

Horn, K. I. 2009. *Roads to Wisdom: Conversations with Ten Nobel Laureates in Economics*. Cheltenham: Elgar.

Howey, R. 1973. "The Origins of Marginalism". In R. D. C. Black, A. W. Coats & C. Goodwin (eds), *The Marginal Revolution in Economics: Interpretation and Evaluation*, pp. 15–36. Durham, NC: Duke University Press.

Hudson, K. 2012. *The New European Left: A Socialism for the Twenty-First Century?* Basingstoke: Palgrave Macmillan.

Hughes, C. 2011. *Liberal Democracy as the End of History: Fukuyama and Postmodern Challenges*. London: Routledge.

Humphery, K. 1998. *Shelf Life: Supermarkets and the Changing Cultures of Consumption*. Cambridge: Cambridge University Press.

Humphrey, T. 1992. "Marshallian cross diagrams and their uses before Alfred Marshall: the origins of supply and demand geometry", *Federal Reserve Bank of Richmond Economic Review* 78:2, pp. 3–22.

Humphrey, T. 2010. "Marshallian Cross Diagrams". In M. Blaug & P. Lloyd (eds), *Famous Figures and Diagrams in Economics*, pp. 29–37. Cheltenham: Elgar.

Hutton, W. 2001. *The Revolution that Never Was: An Assessment of Keynesian Economics*, new edition. London: Vintage.

Ingrao, B. & G. Israel 1990. *The Invisible Hand: Economic Equilibrium in the History of Science*, trans. I. McGilvray. Cambridge, MA: MIT Press.

Jaffé, W. 1967. "Walras' theory of *tâtonnement*: a critique of recent interpretations", *Journal of Political Economy* 75:1, pp. 1–19.

Jehle, G. & P. Reny 2001. *Advanced Microeconomic Theory*, second edition. Boston, MA: Addison Wesley.

Jenkin, F. 2014 [1868]. "Trade-Unions: How Far Legitimate". In S. Colvin & J. A. Ewing (eds), *Fleeming Jenkin: Papers, Literary, Scientific, etc: Vol. 2*, pp. 3–75. Cambridge: Cambridge University Press, 2014 [1877].

Jenkin, F. 2014 [1870]. "The Graphic Representation of the Laws of Supply and Demand, and Their Application to Labour". In S. Colvin & J. A. Ewing (eds), *Fleeming Jenkin: Papers, Literary, Scientific, etc: Vol. 2*, pp. 76–106. Cambridge: Cambridge University Press, 2014 [1877].

Jenkin, F. 2014 [1872]. "On the Principles which Regulate the Incidence of Taxes". In S. Colvin & J. A. Ewing (eds), *Fleeming Jenkin: Papers, Literary, Scientific, etc: Vol. 2*, pp. 107–21. Cambridge: Cambridge University Press, 2014 [1877].

Jevons, W. S. 2013 [1871/1888]. *The Theory of Political Economy*, composite of the first, second and third editions. Basingstoke: Palgrave Macmillan.

Jevons, W. S. 2013 [1871]. "Preface to the First Edition". In W. S. Jevons, *The Theory of Political Economy*, composite of the first, second and third editions, pp. xxvii–xxxi. Basingstoke: Palgrave Macmillan, 2013 [1871/1888].

Jevons, W. S. 2013 [1879]. "Preface to the Second Edition". In W. S. Jevons, *The Theory of Political Economy*, composite of the first, second and third editions, pp. xxxii–lxxiii. Basingstoke: Palgrave Macmillan, 2013 [1871/1888].

Johansson, P.-O. 1991. *An Introduction to Modern Welfare Economics*. Cambridge: Cambridge University Press.

Justman, S. 1993. *The Autonomous Male of Adam Smith*. Norman, OK: University of Oklahoma Press.

Kang, D. 2002. *Crony Capitalism: Corruption and Development in South Korea and the Philippines*. Cambridge: Cambridge University Press.

Kates, S. 2013. *Defending the History of Economic Thought*. Cheltenham: Elgar.

Katz, M. & H. Rosen 1991. *Microeconomics*. Boston, MA: Irwin.

Keita, L. D. 1992. *Science, Rationality, and Neoclassical Economics*. London: Associated University Presses.

Kelly, K. 2009. *Street Fighters: The Last 72 Hours of Bear Stearns, the Toughest Firm on Wall Street*. New York: Portfolio.

Kennedy, G. 2008. *Adam Smith: A Moral Philosopher and His Political Economy*. Basingstoke: Palgrave Macmillan.

Keppler, J. H. 2010. *Adam Smith and the Economy of the Passions*. London: Routledge.

Keynes, J. M. 1937. "The general theory of employment", *Quarterly Journal of Economics* 51:2, pp. 209–23.

Keynes, J. M. 1997 [1936]. *The General Theory of Employment, Interest, and Money*. London: Prometheus.

Khatri, N. & A. Ojha (eds) 2016. *Crony Capitalism in India: Establishing Robust Counteractive Institutional Frameworks*. Basingstoke: Palgrave Macmillan.

Kiely, R. 2017. *The Neoliberal Paradox*. Cheltenham: Elgar.

Kim, H.-R. 2000. "Fragility or Continuity? Economic Governance of East Asian Capitalism". In R. Robison, M. Beeson, K. Jayasuriya & H.-R. Kim (eds), *Politics and Markets in the Wake of the Asian Crisis*, pp. 99–115. London: Routledge.

Kirby, M. 2000. *Sociology in Perspective*. London: Heinemann.

Kirman, A. 1989. "The intrinsic limits of modern economic theory: the emperor has no clothes", *Economic Journal* 99 (supplement), pp. 126–39.

Kirman, A. 1992. "Whom or what does the representative individual represent?", *Journal of Economic Perspectives* 6:2, pp. 117–36.

Klein, L. 1968. *The Keynesian Revolution*, second edition. London: Macmillan.

Klein, J. 1995. "The Method of Diagrams and the Black Arts of Inductive Economics". In I. Rima (ed.), *Measurement, Quantification and Economic Analysis: Numeracy in Economics*, pp. 98–139. London: Routledge.

Koetsier, T. & L. Bergmans (eds) 2005. *Mathematics and the Divine: A Historical Study*. Amsterdam: Elsevier.

Kolm, S.-C. 1968. "Léon Walras' correspondence and related papers: the birth of mathematical economics", *American Economic Review* 58:5, 1330–41.

Krauss, M. & H. Johnson 2009. *General Equilibrium Analysis: A Micro-Economic Text*. New York: Transaction.

Kreps, D. & J. Scheinkman 1988. "Quantity Precommitment and Bertrand Competition Yield Cournot Outcomes". In A. Daughety (ed.), *Cournot Oligopoly: Characterization and Applications*, pp. 201–17. Cambridge: Cambridge University Press.

Krugman, P. & R. Wells 2015. *Microeconomics*, fourth edition. London: Worth.

Kydland, F. & E. Prescott 1977. "Rules rather than discretion: the inconsistency of optimal plans", *Journal of Political Economy* 85:3, pp. 473–91.

Lamb, D. & S. Easton 1984. *Multiple Discovery: The Pattern of Scientific Progress*. Aldershot: Avebury.

Lavelle, A. 2016. *The Death of Social Democracy: Political Consequences in the 21st Century*. London: Routledge.

Law, J. 1750 [1705]. *Money and Trade Considered: With a Proposal for Supplying the Nation with Money*. Glasgow: R. & A. Foulis.

le Heron, E. & E. Carre 2006. "Credibility versus Confidence in Monetary Policy". In R. Wray & M. Forstater (eds), *Money, Financial Instability and Stabilization Policy*, pp. 58–84. Cheltenham: Elgar.

Leshem, D. 2016. *The Origins of Neoliberalism: Modeling the Economy from Jesus to Foucault*. New York: Columbia University Press.

Lewis, H. 2013. *Crony Capitalism in America, 2008-2012*. New York: AC2 Books.

Leys, C. 2003. *Market-Driven Politics: Neoliberal Democracy and the Public Interest*. London: Verso.

Little, I. 2002. *A Critique of Welfare Economics*, reissued edition. Oxford: Oxford University Press.

Lipschutz, R. & J. Rowe 2005. *Globalization, Governmentality and Global Politics: Regulation for the Rest of Us?* London: Routledge.

Lipsey, R. & K. Lancaster 1956. "The general theory of second best", *Review of Economic Studies* 24:1, pp. 11–32.

Lohmann, S. 1998. "Reputational versus Institutional Solutions to the Time-Consistency Problem in Monetary Policy". In S. Eijffinger & H. Huizinga (eds), *Positive Political Economy: Theory and Evidence*, pp. 9–22. Cambridge: Cambridge University Press.

Louçã, F. 2007. *The Years of High Econometrics: A Short History of the Generation that Reinvented Economics*. London: Routledge.

Lucas, R. 1976. "Econometric Policy Evaluation: A Critique". In R. Lucas, *Studies in Business-Cycle Theory*, pp. 104–30. Cambridge, MA: MIT Press, 1981.

Maloney, J. 1991. *The Professionalization of Economics: Alfred Marshall and the Dominance of Orthodoxy*, new edition. New York: Transaction.

Mandler, M. 1999. *Dilemmas in Economic Theory: Persisting Foundational Problems of Microeconomics*. Oxford: Oxford University Press.

Mangoldt, H. von 1995 [1863]. *Grundriss der Volkswirthschaftslehre*. Münster: Verlag Wirtschaft und Finanzen.

Mankiw, G. 2016. *Principles of Economics*, eighth edition. Boston, MA: Cengage Learning.

Marcellin, S. 2010. *The Political Economy of Pharmaceutical Patents: US Sectional Interests and the African Group at the WTO*. Aldershot: Ashgate.

Marchionatti, R. & M. Cedrini 2017. *Economics as Social Science: Economics Imperialism and the Challenge of Interdisciplinarity*. London: Routledge.

Marshall, A. 1975 [1870]. "Essay on Value". In J. Whitaker (ed.), *The Early Economic Writings of Alfred Marshall, 1867-1890: Vol 1*, pp. 119–59. London: Macmillan, 1975.

Marshall, A. 2013 [1890/1920]. *Principles of Economics*, eighth edition. Basingstoke: Palgrave Macmillan.

Marshall, A. 2013 [1890]. "Preface to the First Edition". In A. Marshall, *Principles of Economics*, eighth edition, pp. xix–xxiii. Basingstoke: Palgrave Macmillan.

Martell, L. 2010. *The Sociology of Globalization*. Cambridge: Polity.

Martín-Román, A. 2004. "Edgeworth Box". In C. R. Braun & J. Segura (eds), *An Eponymous Dictionary of Economics: A Guide to Laws and Theorems Named after Economists*, pp. 63–5. Cheltenham: Elgar.

Mawhin, J. 2005. "Topological Fixed Point Theory and Nonlinear Differential Equations". In R. F. Brown, M. Furi, L. Górniewicz & B. Jiang (eds), *Handbook of Topological Fixed Point Theory*, pp. 867–904. Dordrecht: Springer.

May, C. 2007. *The World Intellectual Property Organization: Resurgence and the Development Agenda*. London: Routledge.

Mazzucato, M. 2015. *The Entrepreneurial State: Debunking Public versus Private Sector Myths*. London: Anthem.

McCallum, B. 1980. "Rational expectations and macroeconomic stabilization policy: an overview", *Journal of Money, Credit and Banking* 12:4, pp. 716–46.

McLean, I. 2006. *Adam Smith, Radical and Egalitarian: An Interpretation for the 21st Century*. Edinburgh: Edinburgh University Press.

McCloskey, D. 1994. *Knowledge and Persuasion in Economics*. Cambridge: Cambridge University Press.

McCloskey, D. 1998. *The Rhetoric of Economics*, second edition. Madison, WI: University of Wisconsin Press.

Meadowcroft, J. 2005. *The Ethics of the Market*. Basingstoke: Palgrave Macmillan.

Medema, S. 2010. "Adam Smith and the Chicago School". In R. Emmett (ed.), *The Elgar Companion to the Chicago School of Economics*, pp. 40–51. Cheltenham: Elgar.

Meek, R. 1974. "Value in the history of economic thought", *History of Political Economy* 6:2, pp. 246–60.

Meek, R. 1977. *Smith, Marx, and After: Ten Essays in the Development of Economic Thought*. London: Springer.

Meek, R., D. D. Raphael & P. Stein 1978. "Introduction". In Adam Smith, *Lectures on Jurisprudence*, pp. 1–42. Indianapolis, IN: Liberty Fund, 1982.

Ménard, C. & M. Ghertman (eds) 2009. *Regulation, Deregulation, Reregulation: Institutional Perspectives*. Cheltenham: Elgar.

Menger, C. 1981 [1871]. *Principles of Economics [Grundsätze der Volkswirtschaftslehre]* trans. J. Dingwall & B. Hoselitz. Auburn, AL: Ludwig von Mises Institute.

Miller, D. 1999. *Principles of Social Justice*. Cambridge, MA: Harvard University Press.

Miller, M. and M. Salmon 1985. "Dynamic games and the time inconsistency of optimal policy in open economies", *Economic Journal* 95 (supplement), pp. 124–37.

Milonakis, D. & B. Fine 2009. *From Political Economy to Economics: Method, the Social and the Historical in the Evolution of Economic Theory*. London: Routledge.

Minford, P. 1995. "Time-inconsistency, democracy, and optimal contingent rules", *Oxford Economic Papers* 47:2, pp. 195–210.

Mirowski, P. 1984. "Physics and the 'marginalist revolution'", *Cambridge Journal of Economics* 8:4, pp. 361–79.

Mirowski, P. & P. Cook 1990. "Walras' 'Economics and Mechanics': Translation, Commentary, Context" In W. Samuels (ed.), *Economics as Discourse: An Analysis of the Language of Economists*, pp. 189–215. New York: Springer.

Montes, L. 2003. "*Das Adam Smith problem*: its origins, the stages of the current debate, and one implication for our understanding of sympathy", *Journal of the History of Economic Thought* 25:1, pp. 63–90.

Morgan, M. 2012. *The World in the Model: How Economists Work and Think*. Cambridge: Cambridge University Press.

Muller, J. 1993. *Adam Smith in His Time and Ours: Designing the Decent Society*. Princeton, NJ: Princeton University Press.

Murphy, A. 1997. *John Law: Economic Theorist and Policy-Maker*. Oxford: Clarendon Press.

Murray, W. & J. Overton 2015. *Geographies of Globalization*, second edition. London: Routledge.

Muzaka, V. 2017. *Food, Health and Hope: The State and Intellectual Property Protection in Brazil and India*. Basingstoke: Palgrave Macmillan.

Negishi, T. 1982. "From Samuelson's Stability Analysis to Non-Walrasian Economics". In G. Feiwel (ed.), *Samuelson and Neoclassical Economics*, pp. 119–25. Boston, MA: Kluwer.

Nicola, P. 2000. *Mainstream Mathematical Economics in the 20th Century*. Berlin: Springer.

Niehans, J. 1994. *A History of Economic Theory: Classic Contributions, 1720–1980*. Baltimore, MA: Johns Hopkins University Press.

Nietzsche, F. 2006 [1882]. *The Gay Science*, trans. T. Common. Mineola, NY: Dover.

Obstfeld, M. & A. Taylor 2004. *Global Capital Markets: Integration, Crisis, and Growth*. Cambridge: Cambridge University Press.

Oxfam 2015. *Wealth: Having It All and Wanting More*. London: Oxfam.

Oxfam 2017. *An Economy for the 99%*. London: Oxfam.

Pareto, V. 1971 [1906]. *Manual of Political Economy*. New York: Augustus M. Kelley.

Parsons, C. 2003. *A Certain Idea of Europe*. Ithaca, NY: Cornell University Press.

Pasinetti, L. & B. Schefold (eds) 1999. *The Impact of Keynes on Economics in the 20th Century*. Cheltenham: Elgar.

Paul, E. F. 1979. "W. Stanley Jevons: economic revolutionary, political utilitarian", *Journal of the History of Ideas* 40:2, pp. 267–83.

Pei, M. 2016. *China's Crony Capitalism: The Dynamics of Regime Decay*. Cambridge, MA: Harvard University Press.

Peil, J. 2000. "Deconstructing the Canonical View on Adam Smith: A New Look at the Principles of Economics". In M. Psalidopoulos (ed.), *The Canon in the History of Economics: Critical Essays*, pp. 68–91. London: Routledge.

Persson, T. & G. Tabellini 1990. *Macroeconomic Policy, Credibility and Politics*. Chur: Harwood Academic.

Peterson, R. 2016. *Trading on Sentiment: The Power of Minds over Markets*. New York: Wiley.

Piketty, T. 2014. *Capital in the Twenty-First Century*, trans. A. Goldhammer. Cambridge, MA: Harvard University Press.

Pilkington, P. 2016. *The Reformation in Economics: A Deconstruction and Reconstruction of Economic Theory*. Basingstoke: Palgrave Macmillan.

Plantz, D. 1964. "Cournot's *Recherches*: some insights on its influence upon the development of economic thought", *Economic Inquiry* 2:3, pp. 195–208.

Pressman, S. 2014. *Fifty Major Economists*, third edition. London: Routledge.

Pullen, J. 2010. *The Marginal Productivity Theory of Distribution: A Critical History.* London: Routledge.

Punzo, L. 1991. "The school of mathematical formalism and the Viennese circle of mathematical economists", *Journal of the History of Economic Thought* 13:1, pp. 1–18.

Qin, D. 2013. *A History of Econometrics: The Reformation from the 1970s.* Oxford: Oxford University Press.

Raphael, D. D. 2007. *The Impartial Spectator: Adam Smith's Moral Philosophy.* Oxford: Oxford University Press.

Rasmussen, D. 2008. *The Problems and Promise of Commercial Society: Adam Smith's Response to Rousseau.* University Park, PA: Pennsylvania State University Press.

Rau, K. H. 1841. "Economie Politique", *Bulletin de l'Académie des Sciences et Belles-Lettres de Bruxelles* 8:1, pp. 148–52.

Rau, K. H. 2016 [1841]. *Grundsätze der Volkswirtschaftslehre.* Berlin: Hansebooks.

Raynolds, L., D. Murray & J. Wilkinson (eds) 2007. *Fair Trade: The Challenges of Transforming Globalization.* London: Routledge.

Razin, A. & E. Sadka 1991. "Efficient investment incentives in the presence of capital flight", *Journal of International Economics* 31:1/2, pp. 171–81.

Reisman, D. 2010 [1976]. *Adam Smith's Sociological Economics.* London: Routledge.

Ricardo, D. 2004 [1817/1821]. *On the Principles of Political Economy and Taxation,* collated text of all three editions. Indianapolis, IN: Liberty Fund.

Richter, J. 2001. *Holding Corporations Accountable: Corporate Conduct, International Codes and Citizen Action.* London: Zed.

Riefa, C. 2016. *Consumer Protection and Online Auction Platforms: Towards a Safer Legal Framework.* London: Routledge.

Rivera-Batiz, L. & M.-A. Oliva 2003. *International Trade: Theory, Strategies, and Evidence.* Oxford: Oxford University Press.

Rizvi, S. A. T. 2003. "Postwar Neoclassical Microeconomics". In W. Samuels, J. Biddle & J. Davis (eds), *A Companion to the History of Economic Thought*, pp. 377–94. Oxford: Blackwell.

Rodrik, D. 2007. *One Economics, Many Recipes: Globalization, Institutions, and Economic Growth.* Princeton, NJ: Princeton University Press.

Rodrik, D. 2012. *The Globalization Paradox: Democracy and the Future of the World Economy.* New York: Norton.

Rogers, C. 1989. *Money, Interest and Capital: A Study in the Foundations of Monetary Theory.* Cambridge: Cambridge University Press.

Rogoff, K. 1985. "The optimal degree of commitment to an intermediate monetary target", *Quarterly Journal of Economics* 100:4, pp. 1169–89.

Ross, A. 2007. *Fast Boat to China: High-Tech Outsourcing and the Consequences of Free Trade.* New York: Vintage.

Ross, I. S. 2003. *The Life of Adam Smith*, reprinted edition. Oxford: Clarendon Press.

Rothschild, E. 2001. *Economic Sentiments: Adam Smith, Condorcet, and the Enlightenment.* Cambridge, MA: Harvard University Press.

Ryner, M. 2002. *Capitalist Restructuring, Globalization and the Third Way: Lessons from the Swedish Model.* London: Routledge.

Saad-Filho, A. & D. Johnston (eds) 2005. *Neoliberalism: A Critical Reader.* London: Pluto.

Samuels, W. 2007. "Equilibrium Analysis: A Middlebrow View". In V. Mosini (ed.), *Equilibrium in Economics: Scope and Limits*, pp. 166–200. London: Routledge.

Samuelson, P. 1941. "The stability of equilibrium: comparative statics and dynamics", *Econometrica* 9:2, pp. 97–120.

Samuelson, P. 1948a. *Economics: An Introductory Analysis.* New York: McGraw-Hill.

Samuelson, P. 1948b. "Consumption theory in terms of revealed preference", *Economica* 15:4, pp. 243–53.

Samuelson, P. 1983. "The 1983 Nobel Prize in Economics". Reprinted in K. Crowley (ed.), *The Collected Scientific Papers of Paul A. Samuelson, Vol. V*, pp. 838–40. Cambridge, MA: MIT Press, 1986.

Samuelson, P. 1992. "The Overdue Recovery of Adam Smith's Reputation as an Economic Theorist". In M. Fry (ed.), *Adam Smith's Legacy: His Place in the Development of Modern Economics*, pp. 1–15. London: Routledge.

Sanderson, S. 2013. *Sociological Worlds: Comparative and Historical Readings on Society*, new edition. Abingdon: Routledge.

Sandmo, A. 2011. *Economics Evolving: A History of Economic Thought.* Princeton, NJ: Princeton University Press.

Sargent, T. 2013. *Rational Expectations and Inflation*, third edition. Princeton, NJ: Princeton University Press.

Sargent, T. & N. Wallace 1975. "'Rational' expectations, the optimal monetary instrument, and the optimal money supply rule", *Journal of Political Economy* 83:2, pp. 241–54.

Sargent, T. & N. Wallace 1976. "Rational expectations and the theory of economic policy", *Journal of Monetary Economics* 2:2, pp. 169–83.

Schabas, M. 1992. "Breaking away: history of economics as history of science", *History of Political Economy* 24:1, pp. 187–203.

Schneider, E. 1960. "Hans von Mangoldt on price theory: a contribution to the history of mathematical economics", *Econometrica* 28:2, pp. 380–92.

Schönpflug, K. 2008. *Feminism, Economics and Utopia: Time Travelling through Paradigms.* London: Routledge.

Schumpeter, J. 2009 [1954]. *History of Economic Analysis.* London: Routledge.

Shaanan, J. 2017. *America's Free Market Myths: Debunking Market Fundamentalism.* Basingstoke: Palgrave Macmillan.

Shackle, G. L. S. 1967. *The Years of High Theory: Invention and Tradition in Economic Thought 1926–1939.* Cambridge: Cambridge University Press.

Shapiro, M. 2002. *Reading "Adam Smith": Desire, History, and Value*, new edition. Lanham, MD: Rowman & Littlefield.

Sharma, S. 2003. *The Asian Financial Crisis: Crisis, Reform and Recovery.* Manchester: Manchester University Press.

Shaxson, N. 2011. *Treasure Islands.* London: Random House.

Sheffrin, S. 1983. *Rational Expectations.* Cambridge: Cambridge University Press.

Shiva, V. 2001. *Protect or Plunder? Understanding Intellectual Property Rights.* London: Zed.

Sikka, P. & H. Willmott 2010. "The dark side of transfer pricing: its role in tax avoidance and wealth retentiveness", *Critical Perspectives on Accounting* 21:4, pp. 342–56.

Sikka, P. & H. Willmott 2013. "The tax avoidance industry: accountancy firms on the make", *Critical Perspectives on International Business* 9:4, pp. 415–43.

Singh, A. 1999. "'Asian Capitalism' and the Financial Crisis". In J. Michie & J. Grieve Smith (eds), *Global Instability: The Political Economy of World Economic Governance*, pp. 8–37. London: Routledge.

Skinner, A. 1979. *A System of Social Science: Papers Relating to Adam Smith*. Oxford: Clarendon Press.

Sklansky, J. 2002. *The Soul's Economy: Market Society and Selfhood in American Thought, 1820–1920*. Chapel Hill, NC: University of North Carolina Press.

Slater, D. & F. Tonkiss 2001. *Market Society: Markets and Modern Social Theory*. Cambridge: Polity.

Smith, A. 1981 [1776/1784]. *An Inquiry into the Nature and Causes of the Wealth of Nations*, a composite of all six editions, R. H. Campbell & A. Skinner (eds). Indianapolis, IN: Liberty Fund.

Smith, A. 1982 [1759/1790]. *The Theory of Moral Sentiments*, from a composite of all seven editions, D. D. Raphael & A. Macfie (eds). Indianapolis, IN: Liberty Fund.

Smith, A. 1982a. *Lectures on Jurisprudence*, from two sets of student notes, R. Meek, D. D. Raphael & P. Stein (eds). Indianapolis, IN: Liberty Fund.

Smith, A. 1982b. *Essays on Philosophical Subjects*, W. P. D. Wightman (ed.). Indianapolis: IN: Liberty Fund.

Stabel, P. 2008. "Public or Private, Collective or Individual? The Spaces of Late Medieval Trade in the Low Countries". In D. Calabi & S. Beltramo (eds), *Il Mercante Patrizio: Palazzi e Botteghe nell'Europa del Rinascimento*, pp. 37–54. Milan: Bruno Mondadori.

Standing, G. 2016. *The Precariat: The New Dangerous Class*. London: Bloomsbury.

Starr, R. 1997. *General Equilibrium Theory: An Introduction*. Cambridge: Cambridge University Press.

Steedman, I. (ed.) 1995. *Socialism and Marginalism in Economics 1870–1930*. London: Routledge.

Steger, M. 2017. *Globalization: A Very Short Introduction*, fourth edition. Oxford: Oxford University Press.

Steil, B. 2013. *The Battle of Bretton Woods: John Maynard Keynes, Harry Dexter White, and the Making of a New World Order*. Princeton, NJ: Princeton University Press.

Steuart, J. 1966 [1767]. *An Inquiry into the Principles of Political Economy*, reprinted edition, A. Skinner (ed.). Chicago, IL: University of Chicago Press.

Stewart, M. 1972. *Keynes and After*, second edition. Harmondsworth: Penguin.

Stigler, G. 1946. *The Theory of Competitive Price*. New York: Macmillan.

Stigler, G. 1969. "Does economics have a useful past?", *History of Political Economy* 1:2, pp. 217–30.

Stigler, G. 1982. *The Economist as Preacher and Other Essays*. Chicago, IL: University of Chicago Press.

Stigler, G. 1984. "Economics: the imperial science?", *Scandinavian Journal of Economics* 86:3, pp. 301–13.

Stigler, S. 1980. "Stigler's law of eponymy", *Transactions of the New York Academy of Sciences* 39:1, pp. 147–58.

Stigler, S. 1999. *Statistics on the Table: The History of Statistical Concepts and Methods.* Cambridge, MA: Harvard University Press.

Stiglitz, J. 2002. *Globalization and Its Discontents.* London: Allen Lane.

Stout, L. 2012. *The Shareholder Value Myth: How Putting Shareholders First Harms Investors, Corporations, and the Public.* San Francisco, CA: Berrett-Koehler.

Suchocki, M. 1989. *God, Christ, Church: A Practical Guide to Process Theology.* New York: Crossroad.

Szebehely, V. 1967. *Theory of Orbit: The Restricted Problem of Three Bodies.* New York: Academic Press.

Tabb, W. 1999. *Reconstructing Political Economy: The Great Divide in Economic Thought.* London: Routledge.

Tanzi, V. 2011. *Government versus Markets: The Changing Economic Role of the State.* Cambridge: Cambridge University Press.

Tanzi, V. & L. Schuknecht 1997. "Reconsidering the fiscal role of government: the international perspective", *American Economic Review* 87:2, pp. 164–8.

Tanzi, V. & H. Zee 1997. "Fiscal policy and long-run growth", *International Monetary Fund Staff Papers* 44:2, pp. 179–209.

Thompson, E. P. 2016 [1963]. *The Making of the English Working Class.* London: Open Road.

Thweatt, W. 1983. "Origins of the terminology 'supply and demand'", *Scottish Journal of Political Economy* 30:3, pp. 287–94.

Tieben, B. 2012. *The Concept of Equilibrium in Different Economic Traditions: An Historical Investigation.* Cheltenham: Elgar.

Tiersky, R. 2003. *François Mitterrand: A Very French President.* Lanham, MD: Rowman & Littlefield.

Tily, G. 2007. *Keynes's General Theory, the Rate of Interest and "Keynesian" Economics: Keynes Betrayed.* Basingstoke: Palgrave Macmillan.

Tribe, K. 1988. *Governing Economy: The Reformation of German Economic Discourse, 1750–1840.* Cambridge: Cambridge University Press.

Tribe, K. 1999. "Adam Smith: critical theorist?", *Journal of Economic Literature* 37:2, pp. 609–32.

Trigilia, C. 2002. *Economic Sociology: State, Market, and Society in Modern Capitalism.* Oxford: Blackwell.

Turk, M. 2016. *The Idea of History in Constructing Economics.* Abingdon: Routledge.

Turpin, P. 2011. *The Moral Rhetoric of Political Economy: Justice and Modern Economic Thought.* London: Routledge.

Udehn, L. 1996. *The Limits of Public Choice: A Sociological Critique of the Economic Theory of Politics.* London: Routledge.

Urai, K. 2010. *Fixed Points and Economic Equilibria.* Singapore: World Scientific.

Valentine, J. 2010. *Best Practices for Equity Research Analysts: Essentials for Buy-Side and Sell-Side Analysts.* New York: McGraw-Hill.

Van Daal, J. & A. Jolink 1993. *The Equilibrium Economics of Léon Walras.* London: Routledge.

van Dalen, D. 2013. *L. E. J. Brouwer – Topologist, Intuitionist, Philosopher: How Mathematics is Rooted in Life*. London: Springer.

Viner, J. 1989 [1928]. "Adam Smith and Laissez-Faire". In J. M. Clark *et al, Adam Smith 1776–1926: Lectures to Commemorate the Sesquicentennial of the Publication of the 'Wealth of Nations'*, pp. 116–55. New York: Augustus M. Kelley.

Vivenza, G. 2001. *Adam Smith and the Classics: The Classical Heritage in Adam Smith's Thought*. Oxford: Oxford University Press.

Vogel, S. 1996. *Freer Markets, More Rules: Regulatory Reform in Advanced Industrial Countries*. Ithaca, NY: Cornell University Press.

Walker, D. 1987. "Walras's theories of tatonnement", *Journal of Political Economy* 95:4, pp. 758–74.

Walker, D. 2003. "Early General Equilibrium Economics: Walras, Pareto, and Cassel". In W. Samuels, J. Biddle & J. Davis (eds), *A Companion to the History of Economic Thought*, pp. 278–93. Oxford: Blackwell.

Walras, L. 2003 [1874/1900]. *Elements of Pure Economics: Or the Theory of Social Wealth* [Éléments d'Économie Politique Pure: Ou Théorie de la Richesse Sociale], trans. W. Jaffé. London: Routledge.

Walras, L. 2003 [1900]. "Preface to the Fourth Edition". In *Elements of Pure Economics: Or the Theory of Social Wealth*, pp. 35–48. London: Routledge.

Warsh, D. 1993. *Economic Principals: Masters and Mavericks of Modern Economics*. New York: Free Press.

Watkin, D. 2005. *A History of Western Architecture*, fourth edition. London: Laurence King.

Watson, M. 2005a. *Foundations of International Political Economy*. Basingstoke: Palgrave Macmillan.

Watson, M. 2005b. "What makes a market economy? Schumpeter, Smith and Walras on the coordination problem", *New Political Economy* 10:2, pp. 143–61.

Watson, M. 2007. "Trade justice and individual consumption choices: Adam Smith's spectator theory and the moral constitution of the fair trade consumer", *European Journal of International Relations* 13:2, pp. 263–88.

Watson, M. 2014. *Uneconomic Economics and the Crisis of the Model World*. Basingstoke: Palgrave Macmillan.

Watson, M. & C. Hay 2003. "The discourse of globalization and the logic of no alternative: rendering the contingent necessary in the political economy of New Labour", *Policy and Politics* 31:3, pp. 289–305.

Weinstein, J. R. 2006. "Sympathy, difference, and education: social unity in the work of Adam Smith", *Economics and Philosophy* 22:1, pp. 1–33.

Weintraub, R. 1985. *General Equilibrium Analysis: Studies in Appraisal*. Cambridge: Cambridge University Press.

Weintraub, R. 1991. *Stabilizing Dynamics: Constructing Economic Knowledge*. Cambridge: Cambridge University Press.

Weintraub, R. 2002. *How Economics Became a Mathematical Science*. Durham, NC: Duke University Press.

Weintraub, R. & T. Gayer 2001. "Equilibrium proofmaking", *Journal of the History of Economic Thought* 23:4, pp. 421–42.

Westland, C. 2015. *Structural Equation Models: From Paths to Networks*. New York: Springer.

Whitaker, J. 1982. "The emergence of Marshall's period analysis", *Eastern Economic Journal* 8:1, pp. 15–29.

White, M. 1996. "No Matter of Regret: The Cambridge Critique(s) of Jevons's 'Hedonics'". In P. Groenewegen (ed.), *Economics and Ethics?*, pp. 103–20. London: Routledge.

Williams, C. & S. Nadin 2013. "Beyond the entrepreneur as a heroic figurehead of capitalism: re-representing the lived practices of entrepreneurs", *Entrepreneurship and Regional Development* 25:7/8, pp. 552–68.

Winch, D. 1978. *Adam Smith's Politics: An Essay in Historiographic Revision*. Cambridge: Cambridge University Press.

Winch, D. 1997. "Adam Smith's problems and ours", *Scottish Journal of Political Economy* 44:4, pp. 384–402.

Winn, J. (ed.) 2006. *Consumer Protection in the Age of the "Information Economy"*. Aldershot: Ashgate.

Zweig, M. 2005. "Class as a Question in Economics". In J. Russo & S. L. Linkon (eds), *New Working-Class Studies*, pp. 98–110. Ithaca, NY: Cornell University Press.

INDEX